TRUCKS & TRUCKING

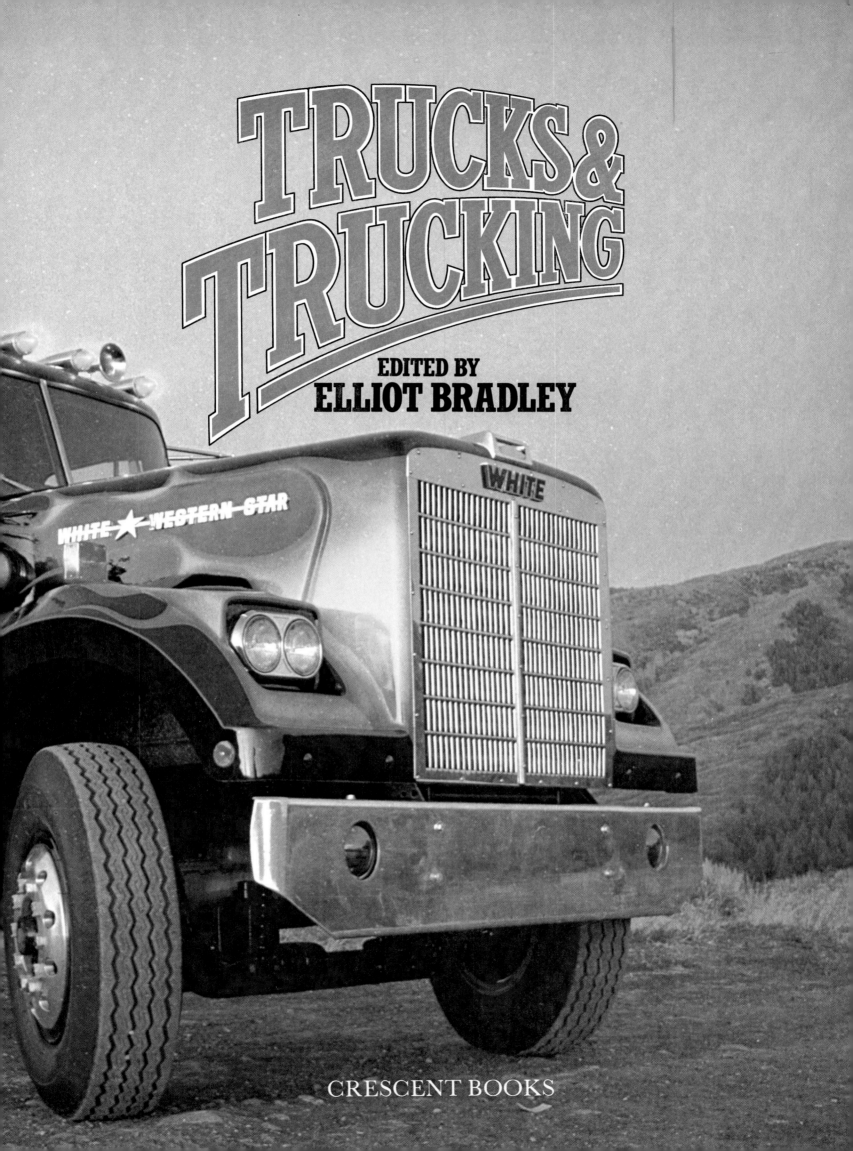

TRUCKS & TRUCKING

EDITED BY
ELLIOT BRADLEY

CRESCENT BOOKS

Endpapers: A French-built Saviem delivers its
load of containers to the dockside.
Half-title: Rigid trucks are the most common
goods vehicles on British motorways.
Title: The White Western Star illustrates the
cosmetic styling of modern American trucks.
This page: Whether it is a house or a multi-lane
highway bridge that is under construction,
materials are brought by the truckload.

First English Edition published 1979 by
Octopus Books Limited
59 Grosvenor Street, London W1

© MCMLXXIX Octopus Books Limited

Library of Congress Catalog Card Number: 78-21697
ISBN: 0-517 27343 8

This edition is published by Crescent Books, a division
of Crown Publishers, Inc.
a b c d e f g h
Produced by Mandarin Publishers Limited
22a Westlands Road, Quarry Bay, Hong Kong.
Printed in Hong Kong

CONTENTS

THE HISTORY OF
ROAD TRANSPORT

The invention of the wheel rendered the A-frame obsolete. No longer did man have to transport goods on this cumbersome apparatus, dragging it himself or training draught animals to do so for him. For centuries horses or oxen were the prime motive power, but with the increasing industrial and technological development of the nineteenth century their shortcomings became even more apparent: they tire on long journeys, their speed is limited and the number needed to transport heavy loads reached unmanageable proportions.

Man had always dreamed of a superior form of power. The search for a source of driving energy led to such devices as clockwork-type wound spring motors and the attachment of sails to load-carrying land vehicles, but even a visionary like Leonardo da Vinci, who designed transmission systems and a differential at the end of the 15th century, could not link his inventions to a suitable power source.

The idea of an invisible source of energy was considered impossible, indeed even sacrilegious, throughout the Middle Ages, and the wildest schemes of inventors and forward thinkers did not always guarantee their social acceptability. Certainly as late as the advent of the steam age, experimenters were often persecuted and had to work in secret. One seventeenth-century Frenchman was confined to a lunatic asylum because of public disquiet about his work.

The French authorities banned horseless carriages on hearsay evi-

This restored Foden steam tractor is shown participating in an historic vehicle rally. Until the 1930s such vehicles represented the British approach to road haulage.

7

dence, and wherever the inventors worked, they and their machines were subjected to stone-throwing and sabotage by a populace alarmed at the noise, smoke and steam of the new machines.

From the earliest experiments with self-propulsion to the full acceptance of road vehicles, the development of the horseless carriage was dependent on the individual efforts of engineers from several countries. The principles of locomotion established by the Scotsmen, Watt and Murdock, and their English neighbours, Savory and Newcomen, were first adapted to road transport by a Frenchman, Nicholas Cugnot. In 1765, Cugnot built a steam-driven gun carriage for the French army which, as the first recorded self-propelled road vehicle, has been universally accepted as a symbol of the dawn of the modern age. The three-wheeled vehicle had a great load-carrying potential, but it failed to impress the army, which suffered from debilitating conservatism, and although Cugnot continued to develop the machine, his career was ruined.

In 1788, the first British steam coach for the carriage of passengers was built by Fourners, and was soon followed by those of Trevithick, Griffiths and Gurney. Although coaches were speedy and well patronized, the railways were getting more positive attention due to their higher speeds and less erratic performance. Almost immediately hostility was directed towards steam road vehicles from many sections of the community, particularly in Britain where legislation known as 'The Red Flag Act' was passed in the early 1860s. This laid down a maximum speed limit and stipulated a minimum crew of three, one of which was to walk in front of the vehicle waving a red flag. The Act also limited steamers to night driving on turnpike roads and so the development of a steam transport system was effectively crippled. The 19th century was the age of railway expansion, and the use of steam locomotives on the roads was generally restricted to agricultural vehicles.

Elsewhere work had been going on into the development of other sources of motive power. During the 1850s, the Italians Barsanti and Mattenici had begun work on an internal combustion engine, while in France Lenoir was developing the gas engine. In 1876, at the Philadelphia Centennial Exhibition, the first American internal

Dr. Church's ornate steam coach (*above*) was built in Birmingham in 1833 and ran between there and London. Passengers had to contend with the elements in addition to a bumpy ride. The Mack brothers built their first truck in 1905. This one (*below*) is one of that generation, now restored to its former glory.

The first articulated vehicle was the British Thornycroft *(top right)* built in 1897. It was steam powered. The Swiss-made Saurer *(centre right)* was an early success in the United States of America. The 5-ton Mack *(below right)* was one of the first Cab-Over-Engine designs.

combustion engine was exhibited by Brayton alongside several European variations.

While Britain steamed on behind men with red flags, the rest of the world had stolen a march on her. The flag was excluded from the Act in 1876 and the other restrictions were lifted twenty years later, by which time Daimler and Benz had both had motor cars running for ten years. In 1893, the Duryea brothers built the first American car and three years later Henry Ford constructed his first vehicle. These and countless other makes of vehicle were powered by petrol engines, but electric vehicles were also in use by the end of the century, particularly on city delivery runs, where horses were proving too dangerous for the crowded streets. Except for certain short haul applica-

tions, the electric wagons were soon squeezed off the streets by the faster and longer ranging petrol-driven vehicles that were coming into use.

Before the turn of the century, events in the commercial transport world were already moving apace. Daimler had introduced a whole range of trucks in 1896, the biggest of which was a 5-tonner with a 10-horsepower engine. In 1897, the English wagon builder, Thornycroft, hitched a semi-trailer to a steamer to gain a payload advantage, so making the world's first articulated vehicle. Five years later the company succumbed to the advantages of liquid fuel and produced a 4-ton petrol-engine truck. In Switzerland Saurer, makers of quality machinery, had built a large motor truck for their own transport needs by 1900, the year in which the Mack

brothers' first bus appeared in America. In 1905, the year that Mack produced their first truck, the Saurer was already fitted with air-compression brakes and, after its exhibition in New York in 1908, the Swiss truck was imported and later built in America under licence.

By the end of the first decade truck builders were cropping up all over the east and west coast states of America, and in Europe, where Fiat built their first truck, a 24-bhp model in 1904. In England, the Lancashire Steam Motor Company was renamed Leyland Motors in 1907, the same year that a merger of American agricultural equipment companies created International Harvester. The White brothers' first trucks appeared on the scene around that time as did Autocar and other shorter-lived concerns. Most heavy American trucks of the time were built with forward control of the type now known as 'Cab-Over Engine' (COE), although in those days there were no cabs, and the driver sat directly over the engine, exposed to the elements. In 1909, when Packard put their engine in front of the driver, as in an automobile, they began the American tradition of building normal control or conventional trucks. In Europe both normal and forward control models were in use, although the long-nose models were a more common sight before the First World War than they are now.

Several American manufacturers sent their trucks out on long distance runs to prove their durability and perhaps convert people to the idea of using trucks for transport. A Saurer made the first transcontinental journey in 1911, a GMC made a two-way journey in 1916, and various shorter, but no less rugged, journeys were made between important cities in the east and west.

These trailblazing runs — the Saurer was named the Pioneer Freighter — did much for the image of the truck in the eyes of rural folk. Farmers had been among the most die-hard of the horse enthusiasts, since their only experience of motor vehicles had been of the crazy devices that periodically came out from the cities driven by slickers, creating plenty of noise and dust, but contributing little else. Once they realized the work potential of the motor vehicle, however, country people became more open-minded. Construction booms in the cities also brought building contractors into the

Lightweight Model T Fords, like this 1919 version, were based on the successful car chassis. The French De Dion Bouton (*inset*) is of much heavier construction. The model shown is a road sweeper.

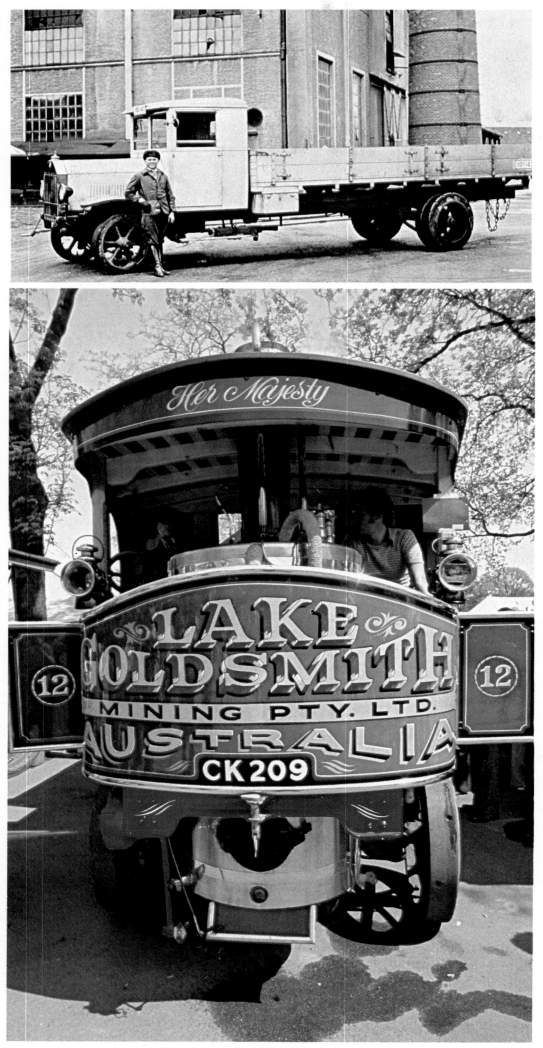

trucking fraternity, and the increasing demands of payload capability quickly led to such developments as dual rear tyres and heavy duty chassis.

In Europe war looked increasingly likely and, in 1911, the British War Office initiated a subsidy scheme whereby trucks were to be built to standard specifications and operated by haulers until such time as they might be called into active service. Among the companies that produced these subsidized vehicles were such famous names as AEC, Albion, Commer, Daimler, Karrier, Thornycroft and Leyland, whose RAF Type proved to be one of the most enduring.

While Britain was involved in the First World War, some American manufacturers came to her aid, including Mack, whose AC model, introduced in 1915, was despatched to Europe in thousands and quickly earned the reputation of being as tough as a 'Bulldog' — a name which stuck. The AC came in a very adaptable range of trucks. Among its unique features was the first all steel cab, which was later offered in a fully enclosed version.

In 1914, Freuhauf began building semi-trailers, the first of which was for fitting to an adapted Model T Ford. The semi-trailer had been seen before in England but had not been enthusiastically received. In America this obvious way to increased payload was readily accepted and Freuhauf led the way in development and production.

One problem encountered by early truckers was the amount of ride transmitted directly through the solid tyres to the load and the driver's body. In 1917, when the Goodyear tyre company began testing pneumatics on long-distance proving runs, they ran their own trucks, often with tandem rear axles and pulling trailers which allowed them to show off a whole collection of new rubbers at once. The advantages were obvious for all to see and trucks so equipped provided greater stability and grip than the solid tyres, in addition to a more comfortable ride.

After the war Britain was flooded with thousands of cheap surplus military vehicles, even though many of them found their way back to the States where the new truck market was also in a state of depression. American trucks had left an impression on the Europeans which influenced the design of future vehicles in several ways. The Macks were object lessons in solid construction, and the FWDs were the first four-wheel-drive vehicles seen in England. They were reconditioned by AEC and trucked on for many years. Semi-trailers had also been brought over by the Americans, and interest in their use was re-kindled. In 1921, Scammell turned out the first British produced articulated vehicle which, thanks to the semi-trailer, could be rated at 22.4 tonnes (22 tons) gross weight.

The petrol engine had now proved itself in the toughest of conditions, but some manufacturers were still looking for other means of power. In 1922, Guy were experimenting with a battery-powered 3-tonner, but the most important event in the evolution of the heavy truck came the following year in Germany when MAN and Mercedes introduced the first diesel-engine trucks.

Dr Rudolf Diesel's engine had been under development at the MAN factory since the mid-1890s, but had been intended only for stationary use. His original design for a compression ignition engine had been patented in 1892, but it took some time for Diesel to discover the advantages of fuel oil. With the support of the MAN company, Diesel continued to develop the engine which, due to its efficiency and economic fuel consumption, found favour as an industrial and marine engine. Once his oil engine had been sold in America, Diesel began to see some reward for his efforts, but soon his mental health began to deteriorate. While crossing on a ferry from Europe to Harwich in 1913, Rudolf Diesel disappeared. There were rumours of murder, but Diesel had made preparations for suicide.

Diesel's engines were used in German submarines during the First World War, but were still too slow and heavy for road use, although MAN engineers continued the development after the death of the inventor. The diesel engine was proving to be more efficient than faster revving spark-ignited motors. It converted more of its fuel into useful energy and ran cooler than the gasoline engines. Although initial costs were high, the intervals between major overhauls could be markedly extended, and the diesel soon proved itself in generators and other continuous running applications. An added advantage was that fuel oil was considerably cheaper than gasoline — in many countries only half the price.

During the late 1920s MAN, Mercedes and Saurer trucks were supplied with diesel engines, and the advantages of the motor were accepted, and soon copied, by other manufacturers.

In England, Gardner unveiled their automotive diesel, a development of their marine power unit, and were followed soon after by Perkins. In 1932, Cummins installed the first US built diesel, a 100-bhp model, in a Kenworth truck. By the mid-1930s most British trucks were offered with optional diesel engines, and many firms undertook the conversion of petrol motors.

In the 1920s there were many other developments in the evolution of the heavy truck apart from the diesel engine — the acceptance of pneumatic tyres was one. Although developed in America, they were first used in Europe by Saurer, once more at the forefront of truck technology. In Britain, trucks using these new tyres could now travel at 20 mph, due to revised speed limits.

Lockheed's hydraulic brake systems were offered in America by White trucks, and on both sides of the Atlantic new manufacturers were breaking into the commercial motor market. In 1929, Volvo built their first truck, a 1½-ton model, and in that

The world's first diesel-engined vehicle *(top left)*, introduced in Germany in the 1920s, caused a revolution in truck design. Steamers like the Atkinson 1918 *(left)* were the mainstay of British production. Many were exported to the colonies. The 1360kg (30cwt) Denis *(right)* typifies the lighter-weight British vehicles of the late 1920s, many of which were run on pneumatic tyres.

same year the Daf company began building trailers in Holland. Dodge had set up a UK subsidiary and Saurers were being made under licence by the British Armstrong company, as well as in France, Germany, the USA and Austria.

By the late 1920s most trucks had electric lights and mirrors and could be specified with enclosed cabs fitted with doors and opening windows. Although cabs were still of heavyweight construction with wooden frames and floorboards, there was an increasing reliance on alloys for engine castings, while steel pressings were being used instead of heavier castings for chassis members. Improvements in gearbox design encouraged manufacturers to use shaft- rather than chain-drive transmissions. To cope with heavier payloads, tandem rear axles began to appear, particularly in America where several firms offered conversions.

While American operators were going for bigger and more powerful trucks, legislation passed in Britain in 1933 penalized the heavies with increased road tax charges, so creating a demand for lightweight vehicles. Those weighing under 2½ tons unladen were allowed to travel at 30 mph on pneumatic tyres, which were by now obligatory on new vehicles. Many older vehicles were to survive for several decades, but the decline of the rail services in America and the expansion of manufacturing and service industries guaranteed that there would be a market for more sophisticated vehicles.

Legislation was also passed on both sides of the Atlantic during the 1930s to regulate the transportation business, which had been flooded at the end of the First World War with cheap vehicles and fly-by-night operators. Those who were running efficient businesses were legitimized, maintenance standards were drawn up and drivers' hours were limited. In Britain the first system for licensing commercial vehicles was introduced in 1933, and two years later the US Motor Carrier Act put road transport common carriers under the regulation of the Interstate Commerce Commission.

From this period the development of heavy trucks which had been running more or less parallel each side of the

Throughout the 1930s and 1940s British trucks became bigger and more powerful. The Scammell (*main picture*) began life as an army gun carrier and was a logical successor to the 1931 Foden (*inset*).

Atlantic, began to diverge. Although increased payload was the common aim, the different conditions in America and Europe were reflected in the style of the vehicles. American roads were generally wider and the hauls longer and faster. In the last years of the 1930s there was a tremendous increase in inter-city and inter-state trucking, and manufacturers were offering powerful gasoline engines in their heavy trucks, which were much bigger than the European diesels. Axle weight limits generated the widespread usage of two-axle semi-trailers and tandem tractors, which in some states could pull double trailers. After suggestions from drivers, several manufacturers, including Kenworth, offered sleeper cabs and

these became popular with the long-haul men.

The light- and medium-range trucks, which had kept many American truck manufacturers solvent through the Depression, had echoed the streamlining of the cars of that period. It was the lighter weight vehicles which dominated the sales figures, but it was the big American trucks of this period which set the pattern of present-day trucking, even though many models were still offered only with gasoline engines.

In England, the heavy haulage end of the transport business had remained the province of the steamer, but in the 1930s these were again limited to a crawling speed on the roads and several manufacturers

changed directly to diesel engines, most notably Foden and Atkinson who adopted the Gardner lightweight engine. Most English lorries, as they were known then, were forward control or cab-over models, although Scammell continued to produce a long-nose model for many years. Six- and eight-wheel rigids were more popular with operators than tractor trailers, and flatbed bodies were the vogue, box vans not being as widely accepted as they were in America. English cabs were still coachbuilt, while the Americans had been using pressed steel for some time. Some American vehicles, like the International D series and Chevrolets, were imported into Britain to have ugly cabs built onto them, in place of the

graceful American body work of the late 1930s. While some manufacturers exported their vehicles to Britain, others set up their own factories. General Motors originally assembled Bedfords from imported parts, but eventually established a complete range of British-made vehicles. Ford also began producing British-built vehicles in the early 1930s and the low cost of these American-designed lightweights ensured their popularity.

During the Second World War, Britain and the other European countries were producing military vehicles and countless thousands were also built by many of the American factories and shipped over under the Lend-Lease scheme. The domestic American industry, however, continued to boom as production was speeded up to help the war effort. As had happened during the First World War, the hostilities stimulated the need for advances in engineering, many of which were immediately applied by American manufacturers. Cummins had produced the first aluminium diesel engine in 1941, which aided the cause of the diesel in a land where many long haul trucks still used big gasoline burners, and Kenworth were soon capitalizing on their experience of building aircraft components.

The immediate post-war years, however, were difficult on both continents, and many truck names disappeared or merged. The transport industry was dependent on the manufacturing industries, and truck manufacturers were caught in the middle. If there was no production, there was no need for their vehicles, so even the most efficient of the new mass-production lines would be of little use. Of the survivors most companies found their new markets abroad. British manufacturers knuckled down to build the biggest and the best of their trucks for export to Commonwealth countries which provided a ready-made market place for the remaining stalwarts of the British industry, and led by Leyland — which began to acquire other makes like Albion, Scammell and AEC — British firms shipped trucks all over the world. Some of the coal burners continued steaming on, but, in 1950, Sentinel built the last for export.

In America, the eventual revival of industry and further improvements to the road system enabled truck makers to offer specialized long distance trucks. As in Europe a number of truck makers went out of business, but others set up, some to flourish and others to fade. Peterbilt had been producing custom trucks on the west coast since 1939, but the most successful post-war American vehicle is probably the Freightliner.

The Freightliner company was formed before the Second World War as a subsidiary of a large freight line, but did not start producing trucks until 1947. The Freightliner, which was later to be marketed by White, was a lightweight purpose-built fleet hauler, of simple cab-over design, and like most US trucks of its time, was offered with a sleeper cab modification.

Mack were offering their big trucks with their own Thermodyne low-revving high-torque diesel engine, while other truck makers were building vehicles with a number of proprietary diesel engine options. The market leaders, Ford, International and GMC, were still primarily builders of lighter vehicles, almost all of which ran on gasoline.

Many of the trucks which were common sights on the roads of America disappeared during the 1950s, and such names as Corbitt, Brown, Diamond T, Wide Track, Federal and Sterling are now memories. Some less traditional designs were tried by various manufacturers who hoped to break new ground or stay alive in such a competitive field. The Fageol Super Freighter was a converted 12m (40-ft) semi-trailer with a cab built in the nose — a truly integrated design. It ran on propane gas and had dual tyres on all three axles, including the front which was fitted with power steering. Fageol continued to build smaller integrated vans, but no longer survives today. The propane engine had also been tried by other manufacturers, including International in 1952, but it was never widely accepted.

The more traditional trucks of the 1950s had become more efficient than their pre-war ancestors, but drivers' conditions had been little improved. Even though they had sleepers, the rough ride, poor seats, cramped leg room, heavy controls and engine noise made drivers' working hours physically demanding. English vehicles were just as uncomfortable, if not worse than the American trucks, but distances travelled were minimal in comparison and there was no thought of introducing sleeper cabs in those days. On the Continent, international traffic was in a state of expansion and most countries were producing long haul trucks, the majority of which were truck-trailer, or drawbar outfits, with tilt-side bodies and canvas tarpaulins, as distinct from the American ideal of the five-axle outfit with box van semi-trailer.

As the building of road systems continued in industrialized countries, the demand for more sophisticated equipment encouraged manufacturers to concentrate on greater all-round efficiency. By the late 1960s drivers were considered essential components of working machines and cab designs began to improve. Cab-overs were still the norm in most countries, and the Scandinavian Volvo and Scania sleep cabs, which were introduced in the mid-1960s, presented drivers with unprecedented luxury. In America, more liberal length laws permitted longer vehicles and there was a revival in the use of long-nose conventional trucks.

Diesel engines were used in almost all European trucks, even in the light and medium ranges, for several years before America made the switch-over. Spurred by legal requirements and commercial considerations, improvements in the basic design of truck engines are continually being made,

and now, in the late 1970s, the trend is towards vehicles which use high-powered turbocharged diesels to move greater payloads in shorter periods. In America, engines fitted to fast long-haul, over-the-road trucks often produce 400 to 600 bhp, almost double the power there was to play with in 1965, while European engines, which are rarely bigger than 350 bhp, have improved as dramatically.

Costs per ton-mile and earning capacity indexes provide the basis for the modern truck operators' financial calculations. More than ever trucks must now prove their efficiency in terms of lower running costs and higher mileage capabilities, often in the face of restrictive legislation.

In America, the main quantity manufacturers, like Ford, GMC, Mack, International and White, are producing 'custom'-equipped tractors, almost off the shelf, in response to the popularity of Peterbilt and Kenworth trucks, which are hand-assembled, using parts from the same range of manufacturers' catalogues. In other areas the big companies have their own specialities. Ford and GMC make most of America's light commercial vehicles, while Mack turn out many special purpose heavy-duty trucks for world markets. Some American independents, such as Oshkosh and Marmon, survive by building for specialist low volume markets, while Freightliner have broken away from current merger practices, and dissociated themselves from White. Most of the US truck builders export a considerable number of vehicles and many have assembly or licensed manufacturing plants on other continents. International has recently gone so far as to acquire a stake in Daf trucks and a controlling interest in the English Seddon-Atkinson company.

On the European continent virtually every country has its own domestic truck industry, with some like Germany and Sweden producing high quality vehicles for many world markets, while the British industry struggles on with the Leyland conglomeration, the multi-national Ford, GMC and Chrysler vehicles, and more spectacularly, the independents Foden and ERF.

Within the EEC many manufacturers have established joint marketing

In the United States General Motors build vehicles of all classes. This heavy duty conventional, the General, was introduced in 1977, and styled to owner-operators' tastes.

and production arrangements with those from other countries. The formation of the IVECO group in 1975 was one of the largest and most successful of these concepts. Under this new banner Fiat and OM from Italy, in association with Magirus Deutz and the French Unic concern, combined to build a range of vehicles with common cabs and chassis units and a variety of power trains. Distribution and servic-

ing were also rationalized, with IVECO dealers able to handle vehicles made in other countries. Saviem and MAN also created another Franco-German relationship with interchangeable components including cabs, engines and transmissions.

A recent threat to the European industry has come from the importation of Japanese Hino and Nissan vehicles through Ireland. Japan's truck makers date back to the 1930s and now produce rugged and cheap vehicles which have the same export potential as their cars.

Eastern bloc countries are also dependent on road transport and have their own domestic truck manufacturers such as Kamaz and Belaz in Russia, Skoda in Czechoslovakia and Nysa in Poland. Some of these are exported to western Europe and many more can be seen in use in Third World countries.

Across the globe trucks will continue to roll for some time to come. Whatever the vehicle, the load or the destination, many of the problems are universal, and although the vehicles may be outwardly different what is under the skin is the result of continuing development to find the most efficient way of moving freight.

THE FLEET

Since the earliest days of road transport the bulk of road haulage and freight movement has been handled by fleets. Originally, livery stables provided customers with horses and equipment on a rental basis. Later some concerns turned to cartage and general delivery work in addition to providing removal and storage facilities.

The first real organization and the basis of a transport system came about with the introduction of the mail-coach, pioneered by John Palmer of Bath in 1784. Fifty years later the Royal Mail began regular services across the United Kingdom, and in the USA, Wells Fargo stage-coaches carried both parcels and passengers. But throughout the latter part of the 19th century most of the heavier parcels and bulk commodities were transported by rail, although in Britain and Europe canals and rivers carried a fair proportion of such goods. With the acceptance of motorized vehicles around the turn of the century many fleets expanded their areas of operation, taking on journeys and loads which were beyond the capabilities of the horse wagons.

In view of the size of the USA, and the great number of communities, it is not surprising that in the United States trucking is the principal method of transport. The USA has more vehicles of all sizes, and consequently more fleets, than anywhere else in the world. The biggest of the fleets are express delivery and general freight operations, usually same-day

This 1937 Albion box van exemplifies the type of 'lorry' which was in common use in British fleets until long after the Second World War. Its smart livery is in the traditional style.

or overnight services, run on regular routes between company depots. The scale of operation can be enormous.

The mammoth American fleets, like Roadway, Consolidated Freightways, Ryder Truck Lines and Mason Dixon, boast several thousand vehicles, but are themselves overshadowed by the US league leader, United Parcels Service. UPS, which operates nearly 50,000 vehicles of all sizes from triple trailer and doubles outfits down to station wagons, is in direct competition with the US Mail for the carriage of heavy parcels which are too small to warrant the extra expense of freight line charges. UPS not only delivers parcels but also picks them up, and all for the same price as the post office's service. In 1975 UPS earned in excess of 1000 million dollars, the first trucking company to do so. The following year that figure doubled. UPS, however, is a special case. It is divided into separate regional companies which are employee owned. Of its staff of over 100,000 most began as delivery men, but on promotion to supervisory or managerial positions employees are offered shares in the company.

The companies which head the more orthodox freight-haulage tables may run several thousand line-haul trucks, but unlike a parcel service they do not make nearly so many pick-ups and drops and work to more rigid schedules. Maximum capacity is their criterion, and although many freight lines operate on a regional basis, they are generally ready to start services on new routes if they can obtain the necessary authority to operate. In America this authority is issued by the Interstate Commerce Commission, and many of the operating rights are still held by the original holders. One of the few ways a fleet can expand its operation is to buy up smaller trucking companies which still possess these 'grandfather rights', which were first issued in 1935. Although routes and prices are controlled, the number of vehicles is not, which is, of course, much to the advantage of the big fleets.

A totally different aspect of long-haul trucking which is also a preserve of large fleets, is the door-to-door removal service, operated in the USA by such companies as Mayflower, United and American Van Lines. These large fleets are run by local agents in all parts of the country and are almost totally operated by owner-drivers. The companies regularly

advertise for solo drivers or husband and wife teams to join them. Finance schemes are operated enabling drivers to purchase their own tractors, invariably cab-over models, while the van lines provide the specialist step-frame trailers.

Other large fleets are operated by private firms who transport their own products and for whom a 40-ft trailer makes an effective billboard on which to display a trademark or brand name. Then there are the specialist haulers who handle frozen food, bulk raw materials and liquids, and indivisible heavy loads, livestock and other loads which require special trailers.

While most areas of the trucking business are dominated by large fleets, figures suggest that up to 90% of the USA's commercial vehicles are operated by small fleets of less than 100 units. To put this in perspective it should be noted that the bulk of these vehicles are small, 4-wheel rigid trucks, such as might be used by city distribution fleets, public utilities and service industries. Most large fleets, except parcel and general freight haulers, comprise a large proportion of owner-operated vehicles which have been leased to the companies.

In Europe the proportion of privately operated vehicles is similar, although there are relatively more smaller trucks to account for. Traditionally, owner-drivers have played a

lesser role in European haulage than their US counterparts, but recently many fleets have begun to take independents on a sub-contract basis to pull company trailers with their privately-owned tractive units. The comparative scale of European operations against American haulage is minute. In the United Kingdom domestic fleets of less than five vehicles account for roughly 65% of commercial vehicles and, as in the USA, the majority of these are light- and medium-weight trucks. Had it not been for nationalization of the larger fleets, with the formation of British Road Services in 1948, the balance would probably also have leaned towards larger fleets. As it is, Britain's largest private fleet, F.B.Atkins, runs 130 tractors and twice as many trailers.

Specialized transport is often undertaken by small concerns which adjust their work load to fit their capacity. If the demand for a fleet's services exceeds its capacity, sub-contract arrangements are made, using other fleets or independently operated vehicles. Larger companies may also sub-contract from time to time, but they generally work to longer term agreements and will plan their vehicle deployment well in advance. If the extra vehicles are needed for a specific period they may be obtained from rental companies on a contract hire

The Bekins fleet (*above*) has been moving furniture across America since the days of horse wagons. The Victorian postman (*left*) is driving one of Britain's first fleet vehicles. Truck rental companies like Ryder (*top right*) provide many of America's fleet vehicles. The tractor-trailer in the background is in the customer's livery. Double trailers (*right*) are used by many fleets, when regulations permit.

basis. In cases where the contract is for a matter of years, trucks are painted in the customer's livery but are maintained by the hire company. Drivers may be supplied by the operator or the renter.

With own-account fleets, known in the USA as private carriers, it is becoming increasingly common for complete fleets of trucks to be supplied by a rental company. Ryder, Hertz and Avis all deploy numerous vehicles in this manner all over the world. While they usually supply from a particular range of vehicles for their short-term self-drive fleet, contract vehicles can be supplied to fit the exact requirements of the customer.

The advantages of leaving vehicle maintenance to the vehicle supplier are basically economic. A large rental company will have extensive workshop facilities and trained personnel, whose expenses will be met out of normal operating profit. The bigger the garage the more chance there is of major repairs being carried out in good

time. Streamlined business practices in matters like parts supply, stock control and computerized maintenance details should lead to a much more efficient operation.

Unless down-time is kept to a minimum, transport can never be totally efficient. Vehicles must be loaded and rolling as continuously as possible. The long-term gains made from successful and profitable deployment of vehicles can often outweigh the added short-term expense of running someone else's vehicles. The confidence inspired by a professional back-up service can allow the hauler the freedom to get on with his real business.

In recent years the organization of the trucking industry has improved immeasurably, although each country has its own particular problems. Vehicles are expected to be reliable and most countries insist on driver qualifications, and stipulate maintenance and construction standards. Regulations vary across the world but the basic philosophy of the transport industry remains the same, whether for a 5,000 truck US freight fleet or a ten vehicle British hauler. The cost of operating must be kept sufficiently low to allow for regular overheads to be met and profit to be made. To the wages, taxes on vehicles, property and profits, maintenance and service costs must be added the depreciation on vehicles and likely effects of inflation and legislation on future expenses.

Initial investment is high. For a top-class full-specification tractor an American operator can expect to pay up to $70,000. For a fleet vehicle the

Even a small delivery truck like the International Loadstar *(top)*, which delivers beer to urban customers, makes a useful billboard. British haulage fleets sometimes operate a variety of vehicles — in this case Daf and Volvo *(above)*. These two makes are the most frequently imported vehicles in the UK. Complete fleets sometimes comprise the Mercedes low profile series like the one shown opposite.

cost might be only half of that. In Europe the equivalent, if less flamboyant, vehicles would not be much cheaper, due to greater inflation in recent years. Understandably the large-capacity freight haulers do not specify top-class custom trucks. They want utility vehicles which are cheap to buy, easy to maintain and economical to run.

The larger the fleet the more likely that its whole policy will be rationalized. Vehicles will probably be supplied by one manufacturer, except where different applications demand a variety of trucks. When vehicles are acquired through expansion of a service, inter-changeability of engines, transmissions, wheels and, to a lesser extent, cabs is advantageous. For a fleet to be able to run a service that is profitable enough to warrant extra investment, the operators must have worked out their ideal vehicle specifications.

As all countries have maximum gross vehicle weights, a major consid-eration is payload capacity, to which has to be added the weight of the vehicle itself. Lightweight vehicles are therefore desirable. Overall lengths are also limited, so long heavy tractors are not appropriate for most highway work, where maximum capacity is obviously important. Every trucker demands the lightest possible truck to benefit his payload capability, but on really long haul operations driver comfort is also a vital factor. Consequently sleeper cabs, deluxe interiors and other extras are specified and so some payload capacity is lost. Largely because of more stringent safety regulations European trucks are much heavier than their American counterparts; often the difference may be as much as two tons on a two-axle tractor unit.

Freight lines normally use non-sleeper cab trucks, which are driven from depot to depot by different drivers who relieve each other at predeter-mined points. These 'slip seat' opera-tions keep the vehicles moving almost continuously. On certain eastern turnpikes in the United States, like the New York Thruway, carriers are allowed to pull an extra 12.2m (40 ft) trailer behind the normal 16.7m (55 ft) semis. These second trailers are delivered to one end of the turnpike by shunters and picked up by waiting drivers, hooked onto a special fifth-wheel bogie and delivered to the other end of the 'pike, where they are picked up by the next shunter and taken one at a time to their destination. The freight line is consequently saving on the services of one tractor for every other trailer. The length of these vehicles would be too much for normal freeway operation, but the straight-through turnpikes carry so much traffic that these doubles ease the traffic flow. In some western states overall length limits allow for triple trailer operations on specified routes, although these are 8m (27 ft) units rather than 12m (40 ft) units and the routes are less heavily travelled.

The shunting process is one which is

American fleet vehicles come in all shapes and
sizes. The White Freightliner (*main picture*) is
a non-sleeper cab, two-axle trailer hauling
double, grain hoppers. The tanker (*inset left*) is
hauled by an International sleeper-cab tractor.
The truck in the service shop (*inset right*) is a
non-sleeper Ford conventional.

common to domestic haulage in most countries. It is frequently used for the carriage of international freight where trailers and containers are often transported by ferry or train without an accompanying tractive unit.

In England during the road haulage boom between the wars, regular night runs were established between principal towns. These hauls were made by the 'trunkers' who would be met on the outskirts of town by local shunters. The trunker would stay the night, usually in some dingy cafe dormitory, and wake up to find his wagon outside with a new load ready for his return to

base. He would set off immediately.

The 1930s were the formative years of road transport in Britain and America. On both sides of the Atlantic legislation laid down the basic maximum hours which a driver could work. In both cases the limit was set at 10 hours per day, although the rest time and total weekly hours varied. Cabs in these days were certainly not luxurious and most drivers were probably happy to step down after their stint and hand over to another driver.

British routes were shorter and the capacity much smaller than in America, so the drivers of the ERFs,

Leylands and Scammells would probably spend most of their driving hours behind the wheel of one particular vehicle, and at weekends or rest periods would clean and check its condition. Drivers who proved the most conscientious would be offered the new machinery as it arrived, although as the industry matured it became customary for senior drivers to automatically step into the new cabs which frequently turned up in the yards of expanding fleets. In American fleets the tradition of the despatcher's board is still observed. Senior drivers are placed at the top of the list and have the first choice of available loads.

Today drivers are rarely responsible for vehicle maintenance, in fact regulations in the United Kingdom and some European countries insist that a properly equipped maintenance facility must be available to the operator. Before granting a British transport operators licence, inspectors may visit the workshop, and will certainly study any contracts for outside maintenance.

The conditions under which the old-time truckers had to labour, which owed as much to the avarice and inexperience of the employers as to the primitive and dangerous road conditions, were awful. Originally faced with restrictive speed limits, like 20 mph in England, and later with limitations on hours, drivers who arrived late received little sympathy from their employers. The schedules they were forced to keep took no account of road hazards or breakdowns. If they were late they risked losing their jobs, and might even be held financially responsible for damaged goods. The attitudes of many employers with regard to preventitive maintenance were also notorious.

As early as 1903 a union was formed which was to become the largest labour organization in the world, although it also earned several other less flattering sobriquets. The International Brotherhood of Teamsters, Chauffeurs, Warehousemen and Helpers of America, rose from humble beginnings in the days when teams-

Containerization (left) is the province of the large shipping companies which own the units. Here two 6.5 metre (20-ft) containers are being loaded onto a 12-metre (40-ft) trailer. Piggy-back trucks like the Kenworths (below) are a common sight in the USA. New vehicles are often delivered in this way to save on engine, tyre and driver costs. Front wheels are removed and axles coupled to the fifth wheel.

ters cranked up the horsepower with whips. It did much to control the exploitation of the transport industry workers by the bosses. Unfortunately while negotiating better conditions and healthy wage rises, the Teamsters frequently became the new exploiters of their membership.

In the late 1970s, despite continuing scandals involving officials, the Teamsters claimed a membership of some 2½ million. Although not specifically a Truckers' union, Teamster members are all involved in the transport and distribution trades. It gives some indication of the scale of the industry when it is considered that, while most freight haulers are Teamsters, there are countless other truckers who are proud to be independent not only of bosses, but also of unions. Estimates suggest that up to 10 million people are employed in the US trucking and distribution industries. The importance of the transport industry in Britain can also be gauged by the fact that the Transport and General Workers Union, with a membership close to that of the Teamsters, is the largest in the country. Again, it is drivers with large fleets who are most likely to be members.

To provide fast and economical transport a fleet which maintains its own vehicles will have preventive maintenance down to a fine art, and will be aware of every conceivable cost-cutting dodge. Large fleets are continually rationalizing their operations, lowering their vehicle costs per mile by judicious spanner work.

Some of the practices of large US fleets may seem only to save a few dollars here or there, but when these are multiplied by the number of vehicle miles they come to thousands of dollars. It is all part of the

continuing battle against inflationary price rises in fuel, parts and labour, increasing road taxes and depreciation of equipment.

Tyre wear is one factor to which any truck operator will give serious consideration. One American freight carrier, operating in the southern states with over 1300 tractors, goes for retread tyres when a set of rubber shows sufficient wear. Whereas most fleets let their tyre supplier handle the retread service, this company worked out that with their turnover in rubber they could more effectively do their own re-capping. In their North Carolina depot they now re-cap 120 of their own tyres daily. Tyres are considered so precious that some fleets cut short the front bumpers, so that they will not be bent back onto the tyre in a minor front end collision. These days radial tyres are much in favour because by creating less friction with the road surface the engine power is more effectively used and so fuel is saved.

Fuel economy is of course the big topic in fleet management. Whatever lengths are gone to to cut costs in the office, terminal or maintenance shop, it is on the road that a truck either earns its keep or becomes a liability. When the oil crisis struck US truck operators were probably the worst hit, especially as it came immediately after the expansion of the early 1970s. Fuel which had traditionally been so cheap doubled in price and fuel consumption was suddenly considered of paramount importance, particularly by large fleets, several of which computed their own ideal vehicles. Suddenly aerodynamics became a major concern. Ryder Truck Lines favoured short-nosed conventionals which were close coupled to trailers, so

smoothing the airflow. They also chose radial tyres. Mayflower Lines, who operated cab-overs with sleepers, invested in a programme of development on the GMC Astro, a wind-tunnel-designed tractor with an aerodynamic roof aid, which they fitted with a fuel-saver engine, clutch fan and various other devices. In Germany, Hapag Loyd sponsored new truck designs as a way to greater economies. Such experiments continue, and any fuel-saving discovery is noted with interest by the fleets, particularly those operating large numbers of vehicles.

Even the largest fleets, upon which might depend a whole regional economy, are small fry in the league of multi-national corporations, but in most countries they are able to lobby governments through the various national associations. Generally speaking, the larger and more established the fleet the more conservative its attitude will be, so in most countries the established leaders often seek the tightening of legislation to protect their own interests. Through such bodies as the American Trucking Associations Inc. and the British Road Haulage Association, fleet owners are able to protest at increased taxes while pressing for better road-building programmes, all the while keeping a critical eye on the performance of the railroads, their supposed arch enemies. These trade associations also negotiate with unions and the authorities on all matters.

The larger companies tend to diversify, merge and set up foreign subsidiaries. For example, Pacific Intermountain Express, an old west coast fleet, has set up in Europe, in competition with existing fleets. Some international haulers, including a group which comprises Ferrymasters, MAT, Seawheel and Norfolk Line, have set up their own trade association which aims to control price-cutting and over-capacity.

In England the largest privately owned international trailer fleet, the Chris Hudson Group, has expanded in another direction with the formation, in 1978, of a trailer manufacturing subsidiary. But, in this respect, America's Consolidated Freightways were first in the field, when, in 1947, they designed and built their own ideal tractor, the Freightliner.

Whatever the political aspects, it is plain that the larger fleet organizations are able to run more efficiently than smaller outfits for a given service, and in these days of massive conglomerates the big fleets can only expand. They are, however, geared up and fine tuned for specific operations, both in the office and on the road. When they need extra flexibility, fleets in most countries find it is often more economical to sub-contract to independent operators.

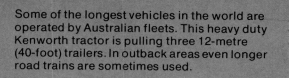

Some of the longest vehicles in the world are operated by Australian fleets. This heavy duty Kenworth tractor is pulling three 12-metre (40-foot) trailers. In outback areas even longer road trains are sometimes used.

THE OWNER-OPERATOR

Among the most flamboyant trucks on the highways of the world are those of the independent owner-operators, the gypsies, who are prepared to take their chances in the fiercely competitive business of road haulage.

Thanks to his personalized rig, and self-employed status, the independent enjoys a unique position. In theory he can choose his loads and destinations. His operating profit can be used to beautify his rig and maintain it to his own specifications. He only runs when he feels like it, and does not have to endure the bad-mouthing of yard managers, despatchers, loaders or co-drivers. He pays no union dues and does not need their support. Although he may make less than a company driver, he is happy in the knowledge that his efforts are not contributing to the wealth of some faceless board of directors. The independent trucker is his own man, with his destiny clasped firmly in both hands.

It sounds like an attractive lifestyle and judging by the number of independents on the roads, it would appear to be a popular and profitable one. But however popular his lifestyle, the owner-operator will have a long hard slog to make it pay. In practice he has to take just about any load that is going, because waiting around for a load means lost revenue. In many cases he will have to take more abuse than the fleet drivers, and while he's running night and day to meet the payments on his vehicle he might wonder just who it is he does work for, himself or the bank manager.

An American owner-operator basks in the glory of his Kenworth W-series conventional. KWs have always been styled with the independent in mind.

In many countries concrete mixers (*above*) are owned by their drivers, but the double-decker tractor (*left*) must be the ultimate dream of many independents. The desire for personalized equipment is worldwide, see the Pakistani Bedford *(right)*.

Company truck drivers from any industrialized country will find little difference in conditions of work whatever continent they haul across. In general, drivers are among the better paid workers, certainly in Holland, Germany and the United States, where they are recognized as skilled professionals. In Britain the same cannot always be said.

Whether or not a driver has a union to look after his interests or an employer to handle the paperwork and maintenance, the driving job remains pretty much the same wherever it is. Only when a trucker takes the plunge and lays a deposit down on a rig of his own will he have to face up to the cut-throat competition, seasonal slumps and operating hassles which beset the transport operator. Because now, in addition to being a driver, he is also a businessman.

Whatever country he trucks in, the independent will come up against a mountain of paperwork, inflexible red tape and a continuing round of bills to be paid for fuel, tyres, maintenance, road tax, income tax, fuel tax, transit tax, insurance, commission and the numerous sundry expenses of the small businessman. Interest to be paid on loans and depreciation on equipment add to the financial burden.

While his exotic machinery may dazzle and impress, the other drivers on the road know that the vehicle itself is no indication of a trucker's success. The chances are that the custom Kenworth with double width sleeper, full chrome and all the extras is a long way from being paid for. The number of very recent full- spec. tractors on the used lots of American truck dealers bear witness to the fact that many owner-operators never stay the course.

The dream of owning one's own truck is as common as any other version of the 'be-your-own-boss' guide to good living. In the rural areas of the USA it is probably one of the most common aspirations of adventurous youth. The difference between trucking and many other adventurous professions is that there is a constant demand for the services of the independent trucker in most countries of the world; without him the less flexible fleets would never meet the customers' requirements.

While it is possible to make a reasonable, or even a good, living as an owner-driver, the road to financial independence is more rugged than any Third World highway. The financial rewards will not be great, particularly when weighed against the hard work, but a successful owner-operator will find other satisfactions in handling his own rig and running his business.

The boat hauler (*above*) has a highly specialized rig, tailored to a particular job of work. Although minimally over-width, this load requires warning signs. The legend on the bumper of the Mexican truck (*left*) is for decoration, as are the many extras.

Anyone who puts up the equivalent price of a new house for a custom-built vehicle has to be an adventurous, optimistic and hardworking individual if he ever hopes to recoup his money. Unless the budding independent has vast resources it is most probable that he will start out on his career with a dilapidated old wagon. He may have several years, experience of driving other people's trucks and learning the business, or may come straight from truck driving school, but whatever his background it is unlikely that sufficient funds will be available to buy a new vehicle outright.

Once out on the highway settled into the seat of his very first outfit, the novice independent will begin adding up experience, filing away useful information for the day when he can order the truck of his choice to his own specification. That day may take years to arrive, but in that time an owner-operator who stays in business will be doing most of his work with

that sparkling new rig in mind. His ambition will be fired, and as the miles roll by the shortcomings of his own vehicle will become apparent. By the time he can afford the deposit on a new truck the independent will know exactly what he wants. Whatever choice is made, it will have to be the best equipment for the job. Although short-haul tipper and concrete-mixer operators are frequently owner-drivers, the main area for independent truckers is over the long hauls, the premium runs, where the distances are long enough to effectively reduce the economic disadvantages of being a one-man business.

The long hauls have proved to be the most financially beneficial to the independent. In competition with a larger concern, he may not be able to match such refinements as computerized billing systems, but he does offer a speedy, direct service to the shipper. While he is on the road he is definitely competitive, it is only his back-up system which might let the owner-operator down. For this reason a reliable vehicle is an absolute necessity. If his rig breaks down or refuses to start, the one-truck operator

will have great business difficulties.

For long-haul application an independent will probably want the biggest and most powerful tractor available. Whether or not he buys his own trailer will depend on the kind of work envisaged — and if the independent trucker does not have some idea of the kind of work he might be doing, then he is probably a little premature in buying a truck.

All trucking demands reliable vehicles and certain manufacturers sell models to large fleets and independents, but the O-O will want more than just reliability. He will want something that is easy to maintain, and as he is going to be driving it for most of his waking hours, and sleeping in it the rest of the time, he is going to demand something comfortable. Then again, the independent is going to be hunting for work from people he does not know, so the truck will have to look sufficiently smart to show his competence. Smart equipment inspires confidence.

Working out on the highways on prestigious runs the independent is going to mix with a lot of really impressive machinery, so for the sake

A new generation of White trucks was launched in 1978. Among the many options on the standard factory paint schemes is the Indian head design featured on this Western Star Cab-Over.

of his ego he will want a vehicle of which to be proud, one which reflects his own character. Just as other ambitious and acquisitive sections of the community improve their homes, personalize their offices, customize their cars, and spend on hobbies, so does the trucker, the only difference being that his rig is all these things and more.

American truckers are expected to display the most splendid custom trucks, but their paint and chrome sparklers are not the only, or even the most outrageous, personalized vehicles. Drivers in less prosperous countries make do with the materials at hand. The Afghans have a reputation for being able to adapt or modify any material and the immaculate gilded imagery with which they adorn their aged Bedfords is a cultural delight in itself.

In Mexico and South America the sleek American conventionals present a more personal image than further north, with drivers' names writ large, as is done in Spain, and religious messages professionally sign-written on the vehicles. Australian 'truckies' take their rigs seriously too, and many of the Kenworths, Macks and Peterbilts down under are adorned with exotic and figurative air brush designs.

Independents in Australia also have the opportunity to Americanize the bigger European models, a cosmetic exercise that is already becoming popular in Europe. It is expensive running an exhaust pipe extension under a chassis and fitting an imported chrome smokestack, but even in inflation-struck Britain, owner-operators are putting that much effort into making their rigs their very own.

The country with the greatest choice of domestic trucks and the most complete trucking culture is the United States. But paradoxically this bastion of the free enterprise system has one of the most restrictive and protective road transport industries in the world. In the USA, as mentioned in Chapter 2, the carriage of general freight is regulated, and strictly controlled, making it virtually impossible for a newcomer to obtain authority to run as a common carrier, which favours the large fleets to the disadvantage of the independent. Fortunately for the independent, and for the American public, who are so dependent on trucks for their supplies,

there are non-regulated areas in which he can operate. Independently owned trucks make up a large proportion of the nation's tractor-trailer fleet, and haul 90% of meat and agricultural produce, the same percentage of steel, and, under various leasing arrangements, nearly half of the general freight.

If the trucker wants the security of regular work which he does not have to chase up on his own, and the other benefits of being attached to a company, he might choose to lease his vehicle to a fleet, as many thousands of American truckers do. At times of undercapacity the independent is courted by fleets of all kinds, from private carriers to the specialist regulated carriers which frequently rely on his services. Among the fleets which offer long term contracts to the 'indies' are the home removal van lines, and in these cases the trucks are painted in fleet livery and the operators often wear uniform. The companies generally finance the initial purchase of the truck, and the operator gradually buys it from them, so while he appears to be a company man, he is in fact an independent operator, with the truck's papers and payments in his own name.

The truly independent trucker in the USA is the one who hauls exempt commodities. As the name suggests, these are goods which are not subject to ICC regulations. Because of the perishable nature of agricultural produce it is one commodity which can be hauled by anybody with a refrigerated trailer. Here the emphasis is on speed of delivery. If a shipper has a load to go then it had better go fast; any delay will ensure that it may be too ripe and consequently worthless.

Almost all the fruit and vegetables consumed in America are hauled by independent truckers. Citrus fruit from Florida and lettuce from California are staple elements of the American diet, and fresh produce is available daily in every small town across the country. Although produce is readily available out of California during the season, the independent who hauls off with a load to who-knows-where must have some idea of picking up a back haul to pay for his return trip. It is no use being stranded several hundred miles from a return load and for this reason many produce haulers only serve an area close to their home base.

To obtain loads the independent either chases up his own business, or

goes to a broker who may supply him with any load which happens to be exempt from ICC authority at the time. The broker negotiates the load, the rate for the job and occasionally pays the trucker and bills the shipper, although more frequently the trucker is responsible for settling his own accounts. In the old days the driver actually bought the loads on credit from the shipper, and sold to the customer, but today the load is generally regarded as belonging to the shipper until it reaches its destination.

American truckers' biggest problems have traditionally come from the diverse and peculiar regulations of the different states, but during the second half of the 1970s there has been some rationalization of the once widely differing rules, although some states have their own fuel taxes, and now demand monthly mileage figures from drivers in order to work out the charges.

The crux of the independents' problems, however, are the restrictive ICC regulations. The arguments for de-regulating the industry are many, as are those of the opposite opinion, but the truckers feel their freedom to operate is definitely hampered by the present mass of restrictive regulations.

One factor which set the truckers' protest movement rolling was the Arabs' oil embargo in 1973, which sent the price of diesel fuel rocketing from around 30 cents to 50 cents or so, almost overnight. Independents took this personally, having to pay for their fuel out of their income. The shutdown during the winter of 1973-74 was primarily a protest at the effects of the oil shortage, and an expression of outrage at what they considered to be profiteering by the oil companies. The truckers' demands were not met. There was no enforced reduction in the price of fuel and the 55 mph limit remained. The independents had made their point, however, and could probably have brought the country to a halt. Feeling was so strong that in most parts of the country no trucks were running.

The organization of the shutdown was handled by the Independent Truckers Association, and coordinated on the highway by the use of citizens' band (CB) radio. Since then other such demonstrations and highway blockades have occurred, both regionally and nationally, and truckers now know they have a way of

Another example of an exotically equipped Kenworth. The VIT designation stands for Very Important Truck. This particular vehicle is in the guise of a wrecker. In the United States of America many of these recovery trucks are owner-operated and they often feature a full compliment of chrome extras. The multi-coloured paint scheme is intended to attract business. Wreckers are frequently converted road tractors and they travel very long distances.

making their presence felt. Such blockades have since been organized in Europe as well, and the leading protagonists are always the owner-operators.

Of the many independent groups which flourished in the USA during 1973-74 most have since faded, leaving the ITA as the principal spokesman for the owner-operator. The impetus for a concerted campaign of lobbying for the de-regulation (or at least re-regulation) of the trucking industry came from the ITA, whose draft Bill was presented to Congress in 1978. The basic contention is that indies should have a right to compete with large fleets, hauling general freight on whatever route they like. They do not propose, however, that the present fixed tariff system should be altered. Flexible rates would mean that the fleets could undercut, as they do in other countries.

American owner-operators may grumble at the faults in their system and bemoan their decreased earning power, but when it comes to fancy hardware they have the greatest and most spectacular variety to chose from. Since the big trucking boom of the early 1970s when there was undercapacity, all the truck builders

have offered specially equipped and decorated vehicles, aimed specifically at the owner-operator market. The thoroughbred Peterbilts and Kenworths now face competition from such suppliers of stalwart fleet workhorses as White, Ford, Mack, GMC and Freightliner.

Sleeper cabs with 1.2m (4 ft) wide mattresses, interior trim kits, extra chrome and paintwork schemes which are as far removed from drab fleet liveries as possible, seduce the impressionable truckers. Prices for a full spec. tractor with mighty turbocharged engine and all the cosmetic flourishes will be around $70,000-$80,000. With a refrigerated trailer the independent will be looking for about $100,000 at 1978 prices. When all the peripheral and running expenses are taken into account it is easy to see where much of the independent's possible $40,000 per year goes. It is also plain to understand why he needs all the work he can get.

The extent of the American truck maker's efforts to woo the owner-operator over to his particular equipment is apparent in the design and nomenclature of all the Powerliners, Cruiseliners, Generals and Eagles, but the most remarkable piece of

European independents have not always had the opportunity to customize their vehicles, so stickers are frequently used. The German Büssing *(above)* is run by a Greek operator.

showmanship came with the launching of a new engine. Produced by GMC at their Detroit Diesel factory, the Double-O 92 is an owner-operator engine (hence the O-O designation) which was introduced in the summer of 1978 with immense publicity. The advertising began by describing the 'sleek charcoal paint with classy gold striping', the flames painted on the manifolds and followed with its bhp rating of '430 horses of hard charging power'. The most outstanding feature, however, and one which the O-Os would readily appreciate, was the 200,000 mile warranty and 100,000 mile recommended oil change interval. An impressive package indeed for an engine which can be installed in almost any new American truck.

In Europe the attention paid to the independent operator has been almost non-existent. Manufacturers have traditionally offered a limited range of engine/transmission options, and until the late 1960s cabs have been very utilitarian in construction and trim. Emphasis on cab design has always been practical rather than

The interior of a double-decker Kenworth cab, complete with all the European options. Sinks and cookers are not common in American trucks, but make desirable extras.

cosmetic and modest rather than aggressively flamboyant.

Internally, the cabs produced by Volvo, Scania and Mercedes in the 1960s and 1970s have many advantages over American trucks, particularly from the perspective of the driver's seat. Leg room and visibility are usually better, while engine noise and draughts are minimized. Externally, however, they have been drab and not especially impressive. Until recently the owner-operator was recognizable by the shabbiness of his truck in comparison with the smarter of the liveried fleets. With the 1960s generation of Scandinavian trucks the driver's image improved and so did the appearance of the vehicles. Once truckers had vehicles they could be proud of they began to look for the personalizing extras and now, although tastes are different, European independents are often recognizable by the smartness of their vehicles.

In Europe the evolution of the various domestic transport systems has thrown up regulations which are often totally different to stateside

practice. In America there are no controls on entry into the industry, whereas most European countries demand knowledge of the industry and/or proof of financial capability. In Britain the licensing authority requires extra guarantees that vehicles will be adequately maintained. Once accepted by the licensing authorities the English owner-driver faces few of the obstacles confronting the American, particularly in domestic haulage. When he hauls abroad he still has to crack the riddle of the international permits and regulations, but in competition with a fleet service the owner-driver's main problem is rate cutting by the bigger companies.

Estimates suggest that Britain has some 60,000 owner-operators accounting for half of the vehicles in small haulage fleets. While these independents are allowed to compete directly with any fleet service, they face various tactics from the fleet men designed to squeeze them out. Fleets will run at unprofitable rates and often continue to cut them in order to retain the business.

During the late 1970s several organizations have been set up to assist the independents. The most

effective of these has been the North Humberside Owner Drivers Association, which in 1978 was a founder member of the British Association of Owner Drivers. The Humberside group was set up as a limited company and shares were offered to the drivers. An office block was acquired and a freight office established to obtain loads and negotiate rates. The Association also helps with the purchase of spares, tyres, fuel and even vehicles, which are obtainable at reduced prices. It is not a co-operative, where resources and work load are shared, but an umbrella organization which protects independents from unscrupulous customers, and helps them get work and keep their vehicles running. Capitalizing on the fact that owner-drivers are more committed to their work, these associations, which are springing up all over the country, are proving to be a vital factor in improving the lot of the independent.

As in any country, when the time and vehicles are their own, truck drivers are more likely to offer a fast and conscientious service. Once they are able to organize their off-road affairs, much of the strain of business is relieved. They can then concentrate on keeping the wheels rolling.

TRANS-CONTINENTAL
TRUCKING

The truck has proved its worth as a fast yet economical means of moving freight and, since the post-war decline in railway systems, roads have formed the basis of most countries' transport policies. International, or interstate, trucking is the top end of the transport industry, the prime money-making hauls being those runs which take drivers on trips of 3, 4 or 5,000 miles out and back, yet necessitate what the Americans call a portal-to-portal service. The increasing 'federalization' of Europe has created a tremendous boom in international trade, with European highway designations linking the domestic motorway systems of neighbouring countries. Since the mid-1970s the spending power and capacity of the oil producing countries has pushed the frontiers of the consumer culture out into Asia and Africa. Laden with heavy equipment, building materials, electrical and domestic goods, modern and antique furniture and all the other necessities of a people who have dragged themselves belatedly into the 20th century, trucks from every European country have turned the Middle East run into a gold rush.

On no other continental landmass will a truck driver be faced with such a plethora of languages, customs, prejudices, prohibitions, inexplicable regulations, and such a complete spectrum of road conditions, from expensive six-lane toll roads to chassis-smashing desert trails. By contrast his American counterpart can comfortably rattle off a 6,000 mile

An Australian road train, with a tractor and double trailers at rest in the desert. Special equipment on these rigs includes the obligatory cow-catcher or 'roo bars'.

A Ford Transcontinental wends its way through a French village (*right*). Modern trucks are scaled to modern highways and frequently cause problems in congested areas. The trailer being loaded with a consignment of grapes (*below*) is about to make a run from Turkey into industrialized Germany. Levels of consumption and international trade have increased markedly in recent years. In Europe, TIR trailers (*far right*) carry goods across many borders to reach their destination. TIR plates enable loads to be driven through customs posts, without the need for inspection at every border.

coast-to-coast round trip in the same number of days as it will take weeks for a northern European to make it to the Gulf and back.

American truckers do not have a completely easy life, of course, but they never need to figure out road signs written in another language, let alone another alphabet. They also have the most comprehensive support from the communities through which they travel. Even if there are scales and police around every corner, the diesel pumps, mechanics and leisure facilities are also just down the road, in a country where truck stops abound. America is not a transit country, a feature it shares with Australia, another massive collection of states, whose variety of road systems might rival those of the Middle East. Brazil,

too, is a massive country, nearly as big as the USA, whose domestic distribution is almost totally dependent on road transport. Until the expansion of the highway system in the 1970s, Brazil's roads were among the most hazardous in the world, and journey times were measured in months.

The most obvious difficulties faced by the international trucker who has to cross the boundaries of his own culture, are those due to differences in language and national legislation, as well as the varying interpretations of international agreements. TIR carnets are documents which apply to loads in transit through Europe. Goods are sealed into trailers bearing the distinctive TIR legend in white on

blue, which denotes *Transportes International des Routiers*. The carnets are checked by customs officers at each border on entering and leaving. To ease the delay which would occur if every truck was inspected, the only inspection of the load takes place in the country of destination.

Each country has its own idiosyncrasies of border policy, some closing at night or on holidays, others seeming to rely on the whims of the officials. And the officers are not always any more favourably disposed to drivers coming into their home country. Often a British trucker can travel up from southern Europe with nothing worse than the usual inefficiency, to be welcomed by the most frustrating delay of all at Dover.

Although the United Kingdom has

hung back on the introduction of the 'spy in the cab', tachographs have been accepted by all other EEC countries, and are required on all commercial vehicles working east of the Channel. The new drivers' hours regulations which were introduced with the 'black box' devices have not only cut down on a driver's time behind the wheel, but have imposed a mileage restriction on single-manned tractor-trailer trucks. These rules are being phased-in over stages until 1981 when Britain will adopt the EEC limit of an eight hour working day, along with a minimum eleven hour rest period and maximum weekly and fortnightly hours. The limited workday, coupled with overtaking restrictions, low speed limits,

and the insistence of some countries in banning trucks during holidays and weekends (no trucks can run in Switzerland on Sundays, when they are also banned from the German autobahns), squeeze a lot of hours from a trucker's schedule. If he does break speed or time limits the fact is recorded on the tachograph, which must be made available to the police on demand.

While Britain goes it alone, at the insistence of the T&GWU, without the dreaded tachos on domestic hauls, she also preserves the anachronistic practice of driving on the left. Even though many British trucks used on continental runs are supplied with left-hand steering, driving on the wrong side is not as strange as it might first appear. All other European countries drive on the right since Sweden converted in 1967, but in Italy domestic trucks have traditionally been supplied with right-hand drive, supposedly to allow the driver a better view of the inside of his vehicle as he screws it round the tortuous Alpine twists. Regulations used to require these Italian trucks to be double-manned, but they have now been relaxed.

European weight limits vary as much as they do from state to state in America. Italy and Denmark set a gross vehicle weight limit of 44 tonnes (43.3 tons). While other EEC countries set their maximums around the 38 tonnes (37.4 tons) mark, Britain stays out of line with her neighbours with the lowest gvw of 32 tons (32.5 tonnes). Operators in sparsely-populated Sweden, however, can run their vehicles at well over 50 tons.

Although membership of the EEC assures that member countries can trade freely with their partners, international transport involves more organizational effort than just loading a truck and driving it over a couple of borders. Each country operates a system of permits, which are awarded on a quota basis and designed to protect the domestic transport industries. The allocation of permits to haulers in transit through EEC countries has long been a problem. Permits are issued in blocks on an annual basis, and most often the bulk of these go to haulers who have already operated the specific route and service. Quotas are determined by the amount of reciprocal traffic from the country of the applicant. This has meant that the United Kingdom is the European poor relation. The fact that the UK is not a transit country, except for Irish traffic, means that allocation of permits is low. Occasionally a country will ease up on its permit quotas. In 1976 the French relaxed their rules and awarded eight trip permits to any operator who cared to apply. Over 1,000 British operators made application. The Italian quota was even lower than the French until mid-1977, when they were increased by 30%.

The allocation of permits to British hauliers is handled by the Department of Transport, and as there are only limited numbers available the DOT has to decide between giving them to large established fleets, or spreading them around the smaller concerns. As with many such allocations, those without previous experience often need not apply. As these elusive bits of paper are so comparatively rare it is surprising just how many truckers manage to do any sort of European business at all. The answer is that often they fiddle. Phoney permits are in circulation, and sometimes it is possible to cross a border with a genuine document, yet avoid the official stamp which cancels it for further use. Experienced continental hands talk of using the same permit time and time again.

Another factor which complicates the job of the British TIR trucker is the island characteristic of his country — to get anywhere else he first has to cross the water. Ferries leave the British coast from numerous ports, heading for every coastline country in northern Europe. The most frequently used port for heavy truck traffic is Dover, gateway to Calais, Boulogne and all points south. In 1977 Dover handled some 30,000 commercial vehicles a month, with an annual throughput of over £6 billion in freight value. The modern ro-ro ferries, those where vehicles roll on at one end and roll off at the other at the

When several European countries raised the taxes on transit vehicles in 1978, truckers blockaded borders. Some blockades involved hundreds of trucks and lasted many days, but their efforts were in vain.

end of the crossing, are in service from ports all along the south and east coasts in hot competition with each other and with Dover.

In Scandinavia ferries present more frequent interludes for the truck jockies, with a transit of Denmark, say from Germany to Sweden, involving 3 sea voyages within a few hundred miles.

In America many of these problems do not exist. Coast-to-coast and border-to-border runs are swift and painless, but only comparatively so. Although a network of federal roads covers the country, over which private motorists can freely range, the state ports of entry present the US trucker with traditional border problems. The language may be the same but regional chauvinism and prejudice are sometimes manifest, and the commercial considerations of protectionism are evident.

In a unique system of vehicle taxation, US trucks must be licensed for every state they run through. A

base plate is required for the home state, and if a run is being made across a state line, the second state, unless it has a reciprocal licence agreement, will extract a fee. If an extra plate has not been purchased, temporary permits can be obtained. Unlike the European system these are freely given out to those with, or exempt from, operating authority, although they do cost money.

At most state lines there will be a weigh station at which all trucks must call. Procedures vary with the equipment in use, but generally the scales are driven over at slow speed and the state policeman, sitting in his booth, checks the gross and axle weights of the vehicles. If suspicious of a truck's condition, the officer can call the driver out and have his vehicle and paperwork scrutinized. These ports of entry are a great bone of contention with truckers, particularly regular interstate drivers who come up against them almost every day.

Until the recent moves towards

rationalization of gross weight limits, American truckers faced a bewildering variety of regulations. By 1978 many states had adopted the 80,000 lb (40 ton) standard, although others allow a higher gvw on certain combinations, while several states maintain the old 73,200 lb limit.

As in some European countries, certain states levy a fuel tax on out of state truckers. On a one trip basis a state such as Misissippi will charge on the fuel in the tank, demanding the equivalent tax that would have been garnered had the fuel been purchased locally. When regular trips are being made with licensing reciprocity agreements, figures of mileage and gallons bought have to be kept and sent to the DOT on a regular basis.

Although the American interstate trucker never leaves his own country, except perhaps for short trips into the cultural satellites of Mexico or Canada, he has the opportunity to drive through every possible kind of scenery and climatic condition. The roads are

first rate. The 42,000 mile Interstate network is virtually complete. North-south, east-west and diagonal runs can now be made between major cities and important industrial areas. The rail-road network was never fed by as many tributaries as the Interstates are by county, state and national highways. As each generation of highway builders have created more efficient road systems, so the original routes have remained and alongside them lie countless small communities. These rural towns are all serviced by truck. Food supplies, clothing, raw materials and equipment for industry, electrical goods, newspapers, hardware, liquor, ammunition, and hunting caps all arrive by truck. Anything the locals might produce, whether agricultural or manufactured, animal, vegetable or mineral, will go out the same way. It is a year-round day-and-night operation, and nowhere in the world do the trucks run so consistently and continually. They have been rolling across the country since before the Second World War, and these days a trucker can live his life completely on the highway or at its edge. He only

has to turn off in order to pick up or deliver his load.

Running over such diverse topography, which takes him from snow-capped 14,000 ft peaks into baking hot salt flats, the American trucker soon becomes experienced in all types of driving condition. The northern states are frequently snow bound for much of the winter. During the spring of 1978 a Snow Emergency existed for several months. Conditions on Interstate 80, where it runs through southern Wyoming and Nebraska, are often bad enough, but further north, above the 49th Parallel, particularly on the

route to Alaska, 'white out' conditions frequently prevail. There is very little traffic in the winter months in this underpopulated and inhospitable region, where the roads are built on permafrost.

The Rocky Mountain range presented a formidable obstacle to the old time truckers in their spindly, rattling old wagons, but these days the giant 400- and 500-horsepower motors gobble up the hills while engine brakes and power steering aid truckers down such famous grades as Loveland Pass, or the descent from Straight Creek Tunnel in Colorado. In winter, official

In the countryside of the United States, thousands of rural communities are served only by trucks. Wherever there is a small town the road is often the only lifeline. This Autocar tanker is hauling milk to the pasturizing plant. Road signs (*inset*) for drivers in the United States are clear. In Europe, the international trucker has to cope with multi-lingual signs.

snow chain controls are set up by the highway departments to instruct truckers to fit chains. Often, going up and down across the peaks a driver will be moving in and out of the snow. Chains being expensive, he will find himself stopping to remove them every time the road is clear. Then, on cresting the snow line once again, he has to stop and refit. He might have to repeat this several times in a few hours.

In the summer months the mountain routes still provide hazards for the unwary or unfortunate trucker. Any problems with brakes can be disastrous, and in some states exhaust brakes or engine retarders are legal requirements. On some routes in mountain states like Oregon, escape ramps for trucks are set up at likely runaway spots.

In the middle of America, running north-south in a wide band across the Misissippi river, is 'Tornado Alley'. Climatic changes in the Gulf send twisters and electric storms up into Ohio and beyond, bringing added perils to those on the road. In the winter the arctic winds blow down across the prairies, covering with ice the bridges as far south as Arkansas and Mississippi, and sometimes even freezing the wheels of a parked truck to the concrete.

American truckers have many other work-related problems, but compared to the lot of those in other countries, they have things set up nicely. The quality of the roads and the varied scenery make following the white line a rewarding career, but it is not all open roads and easy runs. Loads have to be picked up and dropped in some of the roughest parts of the most dangerous cities in the world. Hanging around warehouses in New York and Los Angeles, or the stockyards or steel yards of Chicago, may promise plenty of local variety, but these are also the most precarious places to leave a valuable load and a precious livelihood. Thefts of trailers, and even the hijacking of complete rigs, is a problem serious enough to be on the minds of most US truckers. The hazard presented by the criminal fraternity is one which is most strongly apparent in the United States, where trucking has long been a target for criminals of all classes.

One thing the American driver will not come up against, which the European TIR driver will, is the difficulty of dealing with a completely alien culture. After negotiating the bureaucratic hassles of his European neighbours, the novice Mid-East hauler has to prepare himself for a considerable cultural shock. In fact, the northern European trucker might first have to take a trip behind the Iron Curtain before even entering the Muslim world. Because of permit shortages, drivers often have to piggy-back their trucks by train across West Germany into the eastern part of the country, and drive down through Czechoslovakia, Hungary, Romania and Bulgaria. These countries present a bland and uninteresting face to the western trucker, and officials become more of a problem. Bribery is increasingly necessary as communication ceases.

Once into Turkey, 2,000 miles from home, British drivers consider the civilized world to be a long way behind them. The way ahead presents new risks and unexpected perils. A wise driver will have negotiated his rate of pay to include a bribe fund of up to £500 which it is necessary to distribute before crossing Turkish borders. The roads have been improved somewhat since the mid-1970s traffic boom, but they still trace the edges of steep gorges hundreds of feet deep, at the bottom of which lie evidence of terrifying accidents. Local trucks, named Tonkas by British drivers after a make of kids' toy, and the ubiquitous express coaches, scream down the twisting highways, often overtaking on blind bends honking, flashing lights and adding to the mayhem.

Local police are rarely seen unless a personal injury is caused by a foreign vehicle, when they take a very grave view. If such an accident is really serious the total bribe fund may not be sufficient to keep the trucker out of jail. Other hazards include outright bandits and pilfering children who make rest hours as precarious as road time.

Once over the 8,000 ft Tahir pass close to the Russian border, the road runs down towards Tehran and the junction of the Asian highway where a better class of road temporarily prevails. Here the European trucks begin to be outnumbered by Asian and Arab drivers, wheeling a wide assortment of vehicles. Some TIR drivers continue the long haul to Karachi and beyond, but most Europeans turn south, taking the road through the ancient kingdom of Mesopotamia to the Gulf. Even after such an epic 4,000 mile trip, drivers' problems are often compounded by delays while customs are cleared and the vehicle unloaded.

Many vehicles never make the return trip. They may be abandoned for various reasons, including lack of experience about suitable vehicles for such a haul, loss of nerve, or fraudulent intent on the part of a driver or local hustler. So many vehicles go missing that one British ex-policeman has set up a tracing service. He drives to the Gulf photographing abandoned vehicles, making notes of the descriptions and checking through customs records. Many of his clients are rental companies whose vehicles have disappeared leaving little trace.

Challenging the Middle East run in arduousness will be a new route aimed at Nigeria, one of Europe's traditional trading partners. Cutting south from Algiers, the road travels 3,000 kms (1800 miles) to Lagos, Nigeria. The construction of the road as far as the Niger border is expected to be complete by 1980, but even now the Algerian National Road Transport Company is running a fleet of special desert-proven tractor-trailer outfits, which traverse the parched desert terrain, reaching Lagos in about ten days. With Lagos port facilities perpetually clogged up with waiting ships, the route is finding favour with European exporters. When completed in the 1980s the six-day trip will become another prestige run for European truckers who will ferry across the Mediterranean to Algiers.

Although Australian roads are also little better than desert trails, that country has much in common with America, in that the distances are huge, and interstate truckers face some of the same confusion of prohibitions and rules from state to state. The distinctive aspects of Australian trucking are the barenness of the virtually uninhabited interior and the intense heat of the outback. Sometimes it gets so hot that drivers have to rest by day and drive at night in order to conserve their tyres.

Most of Australia's long haul 'truckies' are independents, who, on the really long round trips, may be away from home for up to six months. In some states there are no drivers' hours

Where the roads are primitive, drivers are faced with special problems. The driver of the Kenworth which is kicking up the Australian dust (*main picture*) will be reluctant to stop for any reason. The driver of the Afghan Mack (*inset*) has had a head-on smash.

An Algerian driver (*left*) poses proudly with his desert-equipped truck. The Volvo conventional (*above*) is also a heavy-duty vehicle designed for the rugged conditions of the Middle East. In northern Columbia it is not just sand but swollen rivers which cause the headaches (*below*).

regulations, and in the desert very few traffic cops, so truckers may drive for several days non-stop. The Northern Territories and Western Australia are so deserted that truckies often hitch up as many trailers as they can to their road trains. Triple trailers are usually the norm, although with only nominal fines for being over length, drivers exploit the situation to the full, sometimes running with a total of six or seven 40-foot trailers.

The vehicles Australians drive are American and European top of the line tractors, from Macks and Kenworths to Volvos and Scanias, with a few old British models here and there. Several of these manufacturers have set up their own assembly plants down under. The principal domestic heavy truck builder, RFW, market extra-rugged trucks, costing almost twice as much as an imported model. The RFWs are much used as big road-train tractors capable of hauling over 100 tons.

Desert haul vehicles are usually custom assembled with a mass of extras specified. The most obvious requirement is an air-conditioning unit and high on the list of priorities comes a bull bar, or roo bar. This massive steel bumper gives the truck an aggressive look, but is intended to protect the radiator from damage caused by animals, including full grown kangaroos, which tend to leap out at vehicles. The roads across the outback are very primitive and often barely wide enough for two trucks to pass, yet at night they fairly hum with heavy traffic.

Along with a quality of Americana in the style of the trucks and the life of a truckie, the Australians share the Americans' enthusiasm for CB radio which, although technically illegal, has proved to counteract much of the isolation of these desert haulers.

Less developed countries, in continents such as South America and Asia, present more extreme difficulties, but in regions where there is no highway system the business of trucking is more like that of exploration. Third World vehicles exported from the manufacturing countries are always the most powerfully utilitarian of all models. Where roads do not exist there are no weight limits and massive heavy haulage units with multiple drive are often the only suitable vehicles. Under these conditions, legislation is the least of the truck driver's problems. Delivering the goods in such circumstances is a task which compares with the pioneering obligations of the old timers.

TRUCKING FOLKLORE

Judging by the attention lavished on the long haul trucker by the various 'pop' media, the new-found hero of the machine era has come of age, but truckers have been around for a long time, and have always had something of a confraternity to provide support.

Since the dawning of the motor age, the only true professionals out on the roads in all weathers have been the truck drivers. When the roads were comparatively empty, frequently tortuous, and all vehicles susceptible to regular breakdowns, there was a camaraderie among motorists of all classes which is missing on the characterless modern highways. In those pot-hole blazing days the truckers' knowledge of the road and familiarity with machinery were often shared with the less experienced. On narrow roads overtaking was helped by hand signals when the coast was clear. Between themselves truck drivers had a system of light signals which indicated when it was safe to pull out, and when to pull back in. If a driver was in trouble other trucks would soon pull over to offer assistance. If there was an accident, chances were a truck driver would take charge of traffic control until the police arrived.

Nowadays the blinking, not flashing, of lights is a courtesy rarely witnessed among non-English speaking drivers, although in Britain and America the custom survives. Today's schedules are usually too tight to permit stopping to give assistance, and American truckers have learned to be particularly wary of hijack attempts.

The Autocar dump truck, (*left*) operated by a Californian independent, has been personalized to amusing effect. The Keep on Trucking slogan came from a 1960s comic.

The plethora of garages, breakdown services and police patrols in industrialized countries has also made the offer of temporary assistance almost redundant.

Ironically, motorists today, while being more aware of the truckers' image, are less likely to encounter the diesel jockeys than they would have been some years ago. Although the professional drivers' experience was respected on the roads in the early days, the drivers of the much faster automobiles soon came to resent the smoking, lumbering vehicles which clogged the steepest hills and tightest lanes. The public's attitude to the truck drivers was also restricted by their lack of awareness of the truck's role, and their limited knowledge of the driver's lifestyle.

For over fifty years the trucker was stigmatized by the stereotype of a rough talking, waitress grabbing, illiterate worker, just another low-life specimen who had to do a dirty and unsocial job. In those days there were few working-class heroes, and the intra-union brawling between factions of the Teamsters Union in America did little to improve the image. That these men were doing their job with some dignity, and providing a service to all, was rarely considered by the public or employers. That a person should enjoy the life merely demonstrated how much of a rough diamond he really was. The 'Knight of the Road' only turned up in times of crisis, when the public were in need of his practical knowledge. The rest of the time the motorist considered trucks to be an annoying fact of life on the road.

This ignorance of the drivers' role on the part of the general public is understandable; they did indeed live in different worlds. Although motoring in America was increasingly popular before the Second World War, long distance driving was predominantly the truckers' preserve. The best and cheapest cafes catered for the truckmen, while the motorists frequented the more up-market roadhouses, although experienced travellers, at least, soon came to realize that the truckers probably knew the best places for solid food. In Europe motoring was reserved for the affluent, and class distinction on the roads was even greater. In England the haunts of lorry drivers were looked upon with some disdain by the wealthy car drivers.

Although the pre-war public may not have had much cause to envy the truck drivers' lives, this clique of skilled workers have always considered themselves something of an élite. In the primitive conditions which once prevailed truckers were undoubtedly the royalty of the road, and the isolation in which they worked encouraged them to socialize with others of their calling. Truckmen soon developed their own language which was added to the slang of demobbed servicemen, and mixed with that of social groups such as dockers and railroad men.

In America, the popularity of radio in the 1930s spread the taste for country music among the working-class whites. Songs about the truck driver began to compete with those about the railroad men. By the end of the decade several trucking titles had been recorded including 'Truckin In My Tails' and 'Truck Driver's Blues'.

In the 1940 movie *They Drive By Night*, George Raft and Humphrey Bogart displayed all the machismo of the trail blazing truckmen on the USA's west coast. The casting of two stars familiar for their gangster roles was not surprising. They were tough enough to handle the rigours of early trucking, but also showed that drivers were more than two dimensional characters. Raft demonstrated that truckers could become smart, if unscrupulous businessmen, while Bogart showed they had 'nice-guy' potential.

During the Second World War drivers both on the home front and in the various theatres of war kept their wheels rolling, but across the spectrum of war-time heroics the transport drivers' role was one of the least spectacular. The almost total dependence of the armed forces on motor support meant that only the inefficient drew attention to themselves. The heroes went largely unsung, although outfits such as the Red Ball Express, which supplied the Allies' front-line forces after the invasion of Normandy in 1944, achieved some fame.

Domestic truck capacity had increased during the war, and when peace returned, the truck driver's role became more vital as manufacturers demanded door-to-door instant delivery. Trucks began to choke the roads of America and Europe, where motorists and truck drivers were once again in competition for road space. Truckers

Lavish cab murals like the one above are expensive but eye catching. They are more commonly seen on small vans. The oddly distorted publicity sign (*right*) is aimed to catch the eye of passers-by on a New York highway. To catch the attention of fellow travellers the American trucker relies on his CB radio (*inset*).

were a long way from romantic heroes in the eyes of the public and the drivers became more cliquey. Smoke and noise pollution added to the poor image of the trucking industry, until most countries began to bring in legislative controls during the 1950s.

As the vehicles of the 1960s became more sophisticated and less offensive, so too did the highways evolve, with the American Interstates developing the idea of the pre-war German autobahns. There was now more room for all traffic and the truck driver's

image began to improve rapidly.

Radio stations, which by then covered the United States, began to broadcast special shows for truckers in their midnight-to-six programming, and late night motorists became more aware of some of the facets of the truckers' lives, the loneliness and camaraderie especially. Most of the songs were traditional country and western numbers which utilized the emotive qualities of fiddle and pedal steel guitar and the driving rhythms of bass and drums. The lyrics ranged from the whimsical to the weird.

Charlie Moore and Bill Napier's swing treatments of such songs as 'Lonesome Truck Driver' and 'Truck Driver's Queen' epitomized the emotional struggles of a man a long way from home. The Willis Brothers were another popular swing outfit whose biggest hit was the light-hearted 'Give Me Forty Acres' (to turn this rig around). Injecting his own brand of cornpone sincerity into a string of records, Red Sovine sung the praises of the truck drivers as modest, hard-working reliable characters, who loved kids almost as much as women in 'Giddyup and Go', and who returned from the dead to help stranded hitch-hikers in 'Phantom 309'.

Among the hundreds of truck driving records cut during the 1950s and 60s, many treated the common themes of love, wives, waitresses, coffee, crashes, hijacks and hitch-hikers, while others dealt with amphetamine and beer consumption like Sovine's 'Freightliner Fever' and Dave Dudley's 'I Got Lost' and 'Two Six Packs Away'. Dudley's most famous song, 'Six Days on the Road', helped establish the amphetamine-powered stereotype, which then branded all truckers as 'speed freaks'. In fact the abuse of chemical stimulants was already quite common among American truckers, particularly in the days before CB radio. 'Pinball Machine' by Lonnie Irving highlighted another, less harmful, pastime, while Brush Arbor boasted about the potential of his rig in 'The Trucker and the UFO', and Coleman Wilson regretted 'A Green Truck Driver's First Experience with Radar'. Del Reeves, Dick Curless and Red Simpson were among the many country and western performers to establish a market for truck driving songs specifically among the people involved.

A revival of interest in country music and rock and roll in the early 1970s ensured that many of these songs were re-released or covered by other artists. Commander Cody and the Lost Planet Airmen were largely responsible for bringing truck driving songs to a wider audience, with their songs on the album *Hot Licks Cold Steel* and *Truckers' Favorites*. Later, more rock-oriented groups, such as Little Feat and even the Rolling Stones, were to sing about the truck drivin' men.

At the time of the Commander Cody release, America was experiencing a trucking boom with insufficient vehicle capacity and a shortage of drivers. All over the country posters and advertisements on TV, in magazines and on billboards exhorted young people to learn to drive the big rigs. Many were tempted by the thought of wheeling a big powerful truck across the country and being paid handsomely for it, and the trucking brotherhood experienced an influx of new talent — returning war veterans, conforming hippies, disillusioned college students and even middle-aged businessmen looking for a change of career.

The demands and expectations of these new recruits led the truck manufacturers to increase their ranges, offer cosmetic styling and more luxurious extras. Driver comfort in the cabs of long-haul trucks had been greatly improved since the war. Air-ride seats and power steering helped make the job less physically exhausting, and the styling of the new road burners became ever more impressive.

Speed and power had long been

important indicators of a trucker's status within his own culture, but throughout the 1960s and 1970s appearance became a major consideration. Following on from the hot rod car craze and the later trend for customizing personal vehicles, truck drivers began to take more interest in the look of their rigs. Paint jobs became more flamboyant and chrome extras could be obtained at truck stops and through official dealers. In California the drivers' magazine, *Overdrive,* helped stimulate a pride in the vehicles, which has led to some glamorous and expensively turned out vehicles, such as those of the independent truckers and owner-operators.

Particularly in the States, public relations campaigns were launched to present the image of the new trucker, and consumers were made aware of road transport in the late 20th century scheme of things.

Many women joined the new generation of American truckers, and their acceptance by the old boys indicated the new-found respectability of the culture. One of the unexpected results of the trucking boom was that many husband and wife teams took to the roads which, among other things, encouraged manufacturers to offer wider and wider bunks in their sleeper cabs.

The existence of sleeper cabs did much for the image of the trucker, and when they were popularly accepted in Europe became real status symbols. In Europe, certain trucks had been built with sleepers since before the war, but it was the introduction of the new Swedish-built trucks of the mid-1960s which stimulated the trend. Drivers were now spared the uncomfortable prospect of having to sleep across the engine doghouse of their vehicles. They could stretch out fully and also had room to stow a change of clothes. England, with its short runs and less extensive motorway system, was one of the last countries to enthusiastically embrace sleeper cabs, and at first the Volvos, Scanias and German Mercedes trucks were the only vehicles which could be so specified.

European designers had created a generation of trucks which were very different from the Americans and the visual paint schemes and options were much more modest. With the exception of Australia, the customized chrome and flash American look has been slow to catch on. The European truckers, however, were just as proud

of their vehicles and the way they were turned out. In many respects they were more comfortable than the American trucks, which were considered somewhat old-fashioned in their engineering and over-developed cosmetically.

The CB radio craze in America, which followed the oil crisis, was an important factor in increasing the public's awareness of the truckers' culture. For so long the job had been a lonely one, with only the coffee stops for conversation and the flashing of lights for company. The radio shows aimed to keep the truckers awake with songs, messages, road reports and truck commercials, but the men at the wheel had no way of talking back.

CB had been in limited use by drivers before the mid-1970s when America's speed limit was set at a national 55 mph. The initial need to avoid speed traps brought truckers into contact and they began to use the radio as their own medium. Travelling in convoys truckers provided a challenge to authority by breaking the

The trucker (*left*) obviously feels proud of everything he's got. He must spend most of his time behind the wheel of his Peterbilt, earning enough to keep the family happy. The heavily chromed truck (*below*) shows how a New York garbage collector takes a pride in his job, while the trailer slogan (*bottom*) shows an allegiance to the light side of life on the road.

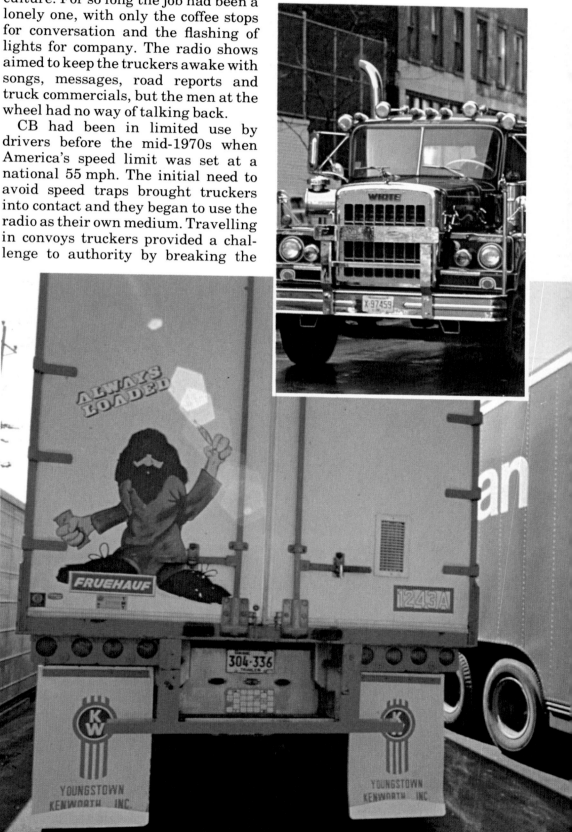

Since the trucking boom of the late 1960s husband and wife teams have become increasingly common on the roads of America. There is undoubtedly much to be said for sharing every hour of the day and night. While sleeper cabs can accommodate two people and their belongings with ease, there is little space for walking a dog.

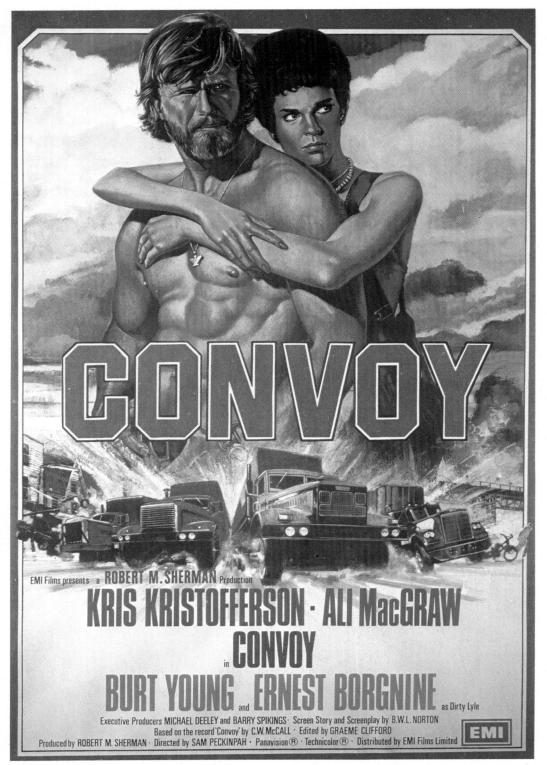

EMI Films presents a ROBERT M. SHERMAN Production

KRIS KRISTOFFERSON · ALI MacGRAW
in CONVOY

BURT YOUNG and ERNEST BORGNINE as Dirty Lyle

Executive Producers MICHAEL DEELEY and BARRY SPIKINGS · Screen Story and Screenplay by B.W.L. NORTON
Based on the record 'Convoy' by C.W. McCALL · Edited by GRAEME CLIFFORD
Produced by ROBERT M. SHERMAN · Directed by SAM PECKINPAH · Panavision® · Technicolor® · Distributed by EMI Films Limited

EMI

solid background and comprehensive mythology. Hollywood movie-makers picked him out for more of these qualities than for the visual effect of his vehicles, although these were obviously important. From *White Line Fever* through to *Convoy*, the trucker has been boosted as an independent free spirit, even though he may be rarely shown to give a damn for anybody's problems but his own.

The generally projected media image of the trucker defines him as a single-minded individual with the solitary purpose of delivering the goods. Thanks to CB, other citizens know he has a sense of humour and, judging by the comments from 4-wheel CB users, his profession is respected. In some European countries CB radios are also used, particularly in Germany and Scandinavia, although in the UK they are prohibited by law. It was the Middle East run, where adventure and big financial rewards could be found, that brought the Euro truckers to the attention of the media.

The range of trucking imagery and media support is vast, and places the anonymous trucker in a position which is unique. The trucking culture embraces a fascination for vehicles and power, where the biggest and brightest is the best, while supporting the pioneering independence of a person who goes his own way and is part voyager to exotic lands and part business hustler. While he struggles on, and in most countries truckers will deny they make easy money, he finds himself envied and idolized by children and youths as if he were an old-time buccaneer.

In his modest way the trucker may have been regarding himself in this light for some time. A card written by Dan Valentine which used to be on sale in truck stops in the early 1960s, extolled the virtues of this character who if born in the past would have been a 'buccaneer, privateer, a freebootin' soldier of fortune . . . a frontier scout, a stagecoach driver', but who, as a truck driver, is 'the happiest and most useful man in America'.

Magazines which inform new buyers of the choice of vehicles have been around since the earliest vehicles. Magazines aimed at drivers and dealing with the wider aspects of their

The movie *Convoy (left)* reinforced the trucking myth, while the chrome and marker lights *(right)* and the CB radios *(inset)* maintained the American public's interest.

speed laws, and organizing blockades and demonstrations. The radios have been put to other uses too, and in the US at least, CB radio's social applications were appreciated. With the tremendous increase in usage, however, there has been a recent influx of maniacs and deviants using the airwaves, which sometimes threatens the practical advantages of CB.

Before the open access channels were so frequently abused, truckers had established a new and vivid language, which incorporated radio codes and new metaphorical slang words into their old vocabulary. Spoken in a style known as modulating, this CB jargon did more than

anything to attract the attention of various media, and quickly elevated the trucker to a place in the gallery of American heroes. Television soap operas began to feature trucks and truckers, and European documentary crews travelled the American highways recording material, as did photographers and journalists from a wide variety of magazines.

At the time — the mid-1970s — America was short of heroes. The Hollywood western was in decline, the war in Vietnam was over and politicians and cops had often shown themselves to be corrupt. The time was right for working-class heroes, and the trucker was one ready made with a

WILLIE MIMS

culture are a comparatively recent phenomenon. The daddy of them all is *Overdrive,* which was started in 1961, and imitated by several other US publications. There are now some 30 trucking publications in America, ranging from the glossy trade magazine, *Owner Operator,* through provincial Oregon and Texas monthlies to the *Mother Trucker News,* an established California newspaper in the familiar underground press format of the 1960s. In the UK, *Truck* magazine was launched in the mid-1970s, and in Australia, Canada and most other countries truckers have their own publications.

Through the pages of these magazines can be witnessed the increasing Americanization of world-wide trucking. That the imagery does work in the selling of trucks is reflected in the paint styles and the high specifications, while imported US trucks find buyers in the most unlikely places. Mack conventionals have appeared in Britain, one Swiss operator runs a Kenworth Aerodyne COE. while a European Formula 2 race team uses a Peterbilt Conventional, a most flamboyant but inappropriate vehicle for the European continent.

Accessory shops, rejoicing in such names as Truckers Paradise, and vehicle customizers have set up in England, where the standard of living will prohibit all but the most financially secure and extrovert truckers from turning their trucks into replicas of the American rigs. At the other end of the scale from £200 exhaust stacks are the many novelties which go with late 20th century cults.

Printed tee shirts and decals originated with car racing and rock music and stretch into most areas of youthful exuberance. European truckers love to decorate their sleeper cabs with stickers, and cab-mounted replicas of Michelin men are also used to personalize their vehicles. Models and toy trucks are aimed at adults and children, and range from cheap cardboard giveaways through 1/25th scale plastic kits (including Jerry Malone's *Super Boss*) to radio controlled vehicles which sell in the UK for over £50. Such novelties as cigarette lighters, belt buckles, cap badges and board games are just some of the incidentals available at truck stops in America and through magazine advertisements in other countries.

Since their introduction in California in the late 1970s, drag race meets have spread in popularity. At these events the competing vehicles are working trucks which race the ¼-mile eliminators in various classes determined by horsepower and the number of axles. In 1978 British truckers had the opportunity to try their paces when a truck competition was run at a drag race meeting in Yorkshire. The American meets are truck only events, which are usually associated with the more traditional truck show contests for such awards as best custom truck.

Some out and out racing trucks have been seen on the American strips, as well as at Bonneville salt flats where high speeds have been attained. A Kenworth named *Liberty Belle* set a 132 mph record in 1975, but the following year this was beaten by Jerry 'Tyrone' Malone's speed of 144 mph. Malone's truck is a much-chopped version of a Kenworth conventional which has a low front end, rear spoiler and 1000-bhp chrome-plated Detroit Diesel engine. *Liberty Belle,* on the other hand, was a basically street legal machine, which towed its own workshop trailer to the salt flats.

Malone is a familiar showman in America. Several of his vehicles have toured the country, including his original *Boss Truck* and *Lil' Boss,* the 1978 dragster version of a near-vintage International. As its name implies, this is a smaller truck than the Kenworth, powered by an V-8

Detroit Diesel. Running under the Thermo King Racing Team colours, Malone took *Lil' Boss* to Bonneville early in 1978, where driver Bill Snyder smashed the previous record by more than 12 mph. After clocking a one-way speed of 159 mph, Snyder achieved an average of over 156 mph, and so recorded a new Open Truck class world record.

There is no doubt that Jerry Malone has brought extra drama to the already exciting world of trucking, although his only European appearance, as of 1978, was a rather disappointing run on damp tarmac at a Detroit Diesel demonstration in Belgium.

A trend among the 4-wheel hot rodders which has burgeoned since the mid-1970s is vanning. Once more emanating from California where vehicles have a recreational function, these exotic vehicles go under the generic category of trucks, and many of the CB users who claim to be truckers are in fact tearaway vanners. While the drivers of the 18-wheelers undoubtedly resent this presumption, it is a fact that many of the vanners try to emulate the big rig jockies and dress up their vehicles with large mirrors, marker lights and even imitation smokestacks.

If imitation is a form of flattery, then truckers should accept it graciously. The more their culture is envied the more their collective image must improve.

Whoever wears the T shirts, they help to promote the trucking culture, as do the cast-metal belt buckles (*inset*) and the items of clothing, such as embroidered patches (*right*) of which a wide range is now available.

TRUCK STOPS

Not surprisingly, the USA leads the world in the range of roadside facilities available to the trucker. Whatever he needs for the efficient running of his tractor, trailer, refrigeration unit or CB radio can be found at a truck stop. Whether it is diesel fuel, a new tyre or a complete engine overhaul, the full-service truck stops which abound in the United States will be able to provide a 24-hour year-round service. The giant truck stops which have been built alongside the Interstates have parking lots which will accommodate up to 500 trucks, while the bigger capacity pump islands can fuel 20 or 30 trucks simultaneously.

For his personal requirements the good truck stop will provide the trucker with coffee and hot food, shower, lounge and tv rooms in addition to wire service facilities, CB and telephone message answering, clothing and accessories store and even transport to the nearest bar. There is literally no reason for a trucker to go further than a good truck stop. At some locations everything can be obtained, from legitimate services to more dubious extras.

But even with all the trimmings, and some go as far as employing topless waitresses, a truck stop is not necessarily popular with drivers. The truck stop is the focal point of American truckers' culture, and an impossible-to-define atmosphere is often more important than anything else. Contributing to this atmosphere might be any number of factors, and although low prices, friendliness, good

One of the many Union 76 truck stops shines out like a beacon, guiding drivers in off an Eastern United States highway, with the promise of food and fuel.

service and strong coffee are high on the list, many drivers have their own requirements. Lady truckers, for instance, will expect stops to have shower facilities for their sex, while drivers far from home might chose a stop where they can expect to meet acquaintances from their own state. A good selection on the juke box or a favourite pin ball machine might be other reasons to frequent a particular truck stop.

When they are closer to home truckers will have a favourite stopping place, where the faces are familiar and the accents the same. Some truckers even hang out in truck stops on their days off, and as so many seem to be country dwellers it is understandable that a truck stop on the nearest highway should become a place to socialize.

Many of the people who work in truck stops are caught up in the romantic adventure which the big diesels promise. Waitresses frequently move from one truck stop to another, if the cliché is to be believed, looking for a driver who will settle down or take her with him. These days it is not uncommon for waitresses to ride off with truckers from whom they learn the skills of driving the rigs. The young men who operate the diesel pumps frequently have their own idea about which truck they would like to run, while the more experienced truck stop staff are often ex-truckers who help fire their enthusiasm.

The truck stop business in the US is a very competitive one, with some 2,000 facilities across the country. With the extensive scale of trucking operations in all areas, most stops are open around the clock. Truck stop operators must cater for the needs of all truckers and there are very few who do not roll through the night. Those drivers on regular routes will know where they might meet some friendly faces, or the freshest apple pie, while others will be content to pull up at a certain distance and roll into the sleeper, whatever the stop is like. Except in high security truck parks, no charge is made to those who sleep in their trucks.

When major Interstate junctions or city limit districts boast several truck stops often in view of each other, it is certain that each appeals to a sufficient section of the trucking populace to be profitable. Yet whatever extra services are offered the truck stops are dependent on fuel sales

The Truck Stops of America chain *(left)* operate in several eastern and southern states. The Shell terminal *(inset)* is in New Mexico. Above is a franchized 76 stop.

for most of their income. They have to lead the truckers to the pumps and hope that they are going to fill their tanks with diesel.

Many truck stops of all sizes have regular fleet customers for whom they provide a bunkering service. Truck stop managers are thus often able to account for high volume fuel sales thanks to a carrier based on the other side of the country whose trucks roll past his facility.

The giant multi-million dollar truck stop complexes with their acres of space and dozens of employees are mostly owned by oil companies, but operated by private managements under a franchise. Most of these are run by individuals or partnerships,

and some of the management companies operate more than one truck stop, sometimes even for different oil companies. The most ubiquitous of the oil company stops are the Union 76 Auto/Truck Stops, the red and blue spherical or circular signs of which beckon to truckers across the country.

These truck stops range from those with only three or four diesel pumps to some of the largest in the land. While they vary in size, however, they must provide certain services to a satisfactory standard. Restaurants will have been vetted for quality, although operators are obliged to organize their own catering and plan their own menus. Wash and shower rooms are regularly inspected, and as is evident at most 76 Auto/Truck Stops an effort is made to attract the truckers. They even publish a free magazine, *Road King,* which accepts contributions

A good truck stop can often be recognized by the long line of tractor-trailers occupying the parking lot, as in this picturesque facility nestling beneath the Rocky mountains in America's far west.

from drivers. The fact that these stops also cater for motorists does, however, cause some resentment among truckers who consider their time too important to be delayed by 'tourists'. Professional drivers do have their own seating area in the restaurants as they do in most truck stops, but truckers frequently need a fast cup of coffee and appreciate the undivided attention of the waitress. Experienced truckers can remember when some of the older 76 stops were run by the Pure Oil Company, and were simply called Pure Truck Stops.

The biggest exception to the franchise practice is the Truckstops of America chain which has 28 truck stops, either operating or under construction, mainly in the southern and eastern states. TSA is a big business with 2,000 of what they call 'the greatest employees in the USA'. Their success is not surprising because the company is a subsidiary of Ryder Systems, who also run a freight line, truck rental fleet and truck driving school, and presumably know the business from all angles. In striving to provide the best service, TSA have a rationalized menu, serving bulk purchased food at a discount. They also offer a discount on a range of other services.

One option which TSA and other truck stops are increasingly offering is the choice to do without the traditional American service station ritual. In marked contrast to European practice, American gas station attendants usu-

Small roadside diners often survive, even when by-passed by the Interstate highways. The European counterparts vary from the cosy French restaurants of the *Routiers* organization (*top right*), to the more spacious service areas, like the one in Spain (*below*).

ally clean the windshields and check the oil. While they are dispensing diesel the pump jockeys generally clean all the glass, including inside the windows, mirrors and lights, check the oil, bump 18 tyres and even empty ashtrays and sweep the cab floor. As the large trucks take some time to fill, truckers often leave their rigs at the pumps, while they go into the restaurant. When the fuelling is complete a voice over the intercom will call that particular trucker to the pay desk. At some stops, if the driver wants to linger, the jockeys will park the vehicle for him, a practice which would find little favour in Europe.

The alternative service offered by TSA is to ignore everything but the tank, and for this the thrifty trucker will receive a discount on his fuel. If he wishes the traditional full service it is still available but at another island. This emphasis on fuel sales is reflected in the various voucher schemes for shower and rest rooms, which reduce the cost of such facilities for purchasers of diesel fuel. With many trucks carrying 200 gallon tanks, both consumer and supplier take a keen interest in who fills them up.

Many truckers, in fact, prefer to stop at self-service stations and only use the larger facilities for drinking coffee and socializing. For this reason each individual truck stop department, such as barber shop, clothing and accessories store and restaurant, must be self-supporting. Occasionally the

truck stop may be a conglomerate of separate businesses which have gathered around a well-established and popular service station, cafe or repair shop. Many truck stops will have lubrication and light maintenance facilities and, while they may offer a limited mechanical service, it is quite frequent for agents for particular engine manufacturers, wrecker services or machine shops to be located at the edge of a truck stop lot.

Alongside the older state and federal highways there are still the more traditional Mom and Pop truck stops which, although in decline, often attract truckers some miles from their routes. While these roads continue to feed the Interstate system there is still some hope for the survival of these small family-operated places, where the service is often far from full, yet where the atmosphere is convivial.

Before the new generation of super highways, the Mom and Pop stops were the only facilities available on the road. Almost all trucks were gasoline-powered before the last war, and one solitary pump attached to any reasonable diner or cafe would be sufficient to classify the establishment as a truck stop. Locations alongside the highway were readily available, and the volume of business required to run such a roadside facility profitably would have been comparatively small. With the evolution of the road transport industry many of these truck stops were able to expand, the only limitation on their capacity being the amount of real estate available for use as parking lots.

With the building of the Interstates in the 1960s, many of the old roadside havens were by-passed. Those fortunate enough to be located close to the

new highways were able to advertise their presence, and where the old and new roads ran parallel they frequently remained visible.

In Europe transport men were just as loyal to their old stopping places, yet when the new roads were built many of the old cafes just disappeared. Advertising alongside Britain's motorways has never been allowed; if it was there would be dozens of cafes and garages within a few hundred yards of major junctions, soliciting trade from the through traffic. As it was, many of Britain's equivalents of the Mom and Pop stops were forced to close. Had some of these establishments been allowed to expand then there would probably have been several full service truck stops in operation by the late 1970s. As it is, Britain has no full service facility and only a handful of truck-oriented service complexes.

Truck stops are so central to the American truckers' culture that the absence of comparable facilities goes some way to explaining why drivers from other countries lack the cultural unity of the stateside truckers. Because diesel has long been readily available in Europe for a wide range of vehicles, it is obtainable in even the smallest provincial or back street garage. On the cramped high streets of some rural French towns the diesel pumps often intrude further into the road than the pavement.

In America, on the other hand, diesel has only recently become widely used, and then almost entirely in heavy vehicles, so many of the truck stops are new facilities. As such, they can ensure they have the necessary space to specialize in truck service. The extent of the country's road system also means that if a truck requires mechanical attention, it has to be dealt with on the spot, or as close as possible. It would be uneconomical to tow a broken-down vehicle back to the yard if that yard was 3,000 miles away.

America's dependence on the motor vehicle has ensured that the country is blessed with an inordinate number of people with mechanical skills. Every small town seems to have at least one garage where temporary repairs and major overhauls can often be effected much more quickly than in other countries. When this aptitude is applied to the vital business of trucking the resulting services are the best in the world. One engine repair

shop which advertises in trucking publications offers a challenge: if a heavy-duty truck is brought in before 4 pm and is not repaired by midnight the company, GMC Desert of Las Vegas, will pay for the customer's hotel room.

While many conscientious garages and truck dealers do exist in Europe and the service does improve, it is frequently the smaller, less significant problems which contribute to delays. Much of the urgency which prompts American service crews, whether working on tyre repair or a serious breakdown, is often lacking in Europe.

The places where European drivers do gather together are not, therefore, often related to the host's mechanical abilities. The places where trucks are repaired are usually far away from any social activity. By tradition, European drivers have the transport cafe as the centre of their culture. Most of these are completely independent from any fuel pumps or mechanics, and the frequently limited parking space prohibits too many big trucks. In their hey-day, before the Second World War, the English transport cafes were able to offer cheap, often home-produced food of high quality; even 'home-grown' steak and bacon was not unknown. Since the war, however, they have laboured under the image of the 'greasy spoon'.

The more recent service areas, regularly spaced at approximately 48 km (30 mile) intervals along Britain's motorways, have come in for much criticism in recent years. These facilities, most of which are operated by leisure or restaurant companies, are integral to the road systems and often offer no opportunity for connection with secondary roads. In effect these service areas have a monopoly on long distance traffic and, as the critics have pointed out, they provide only minimum facilities.

The standard of food at these establishments has been the main object of criticism, but fuel prices are also higher than on ordinary roads, and mechanical services, which are slow and expensive, are limited to certain minor repairs. While most of the restaurants have segregated truckers' sections, many of these are not open around the clock. Although some British facilities, most notably the oil-company-owned Carlisle Truck-Inn, have come close to emulating the all-providing US truck stops, there are none within convenient distance of the

most heavily used international routes around London. Planning permission for one such facility close to Dover was refused on the grounds that existing services on the M2 and M20 roads were sufficient, although none cater exclusively for truckers. In contrast to the true truck stops, most European cafes are dependent on the day-time customers. Breakfast and lunch are often the only meals served in England. Few traditional English cafes remain open all night, except some of those in markets or near ferry terminals.

While English drivers appear to eat only breakfast, those in France indulge in lunch and dinner, which are

only served at the accepted meal times. The contrast between roadside restaurants in France and the English transport cafes could not be more pronounced. In France a network of eating places has been established since the war which gives drivers the opportunity to enjoy the best cuisine.

The thousands of restaurants and country inns which subscribe to the *Relais Routiers* association offer members substantial reductions on meals and lodgings. As the name suggests, the organization was originally intended for truckers, *les routiers,* but proved so popular with motorists that membership is open to anyone, including foreigners. On production of his credentials a member can eat a full meal at lunch or dinner, including wine, at a handsome dis-

Outside America the truck stop facilities are often no match for the massive oil company plazas. On the run to the Middle East truck drivers frequently cater for themselves *(left)* or *(below)* enjoy the local delicacies.

count. The *Routiers* stops are numerous, yet many of them provide limited parking facilities for big trucks, and few are associated with other services such as fuel pumps or garages.

The emphasis on food is typically French, and in restaurants all over the country, meals are only served at formal eating times. Truckers from other European countries frequently become members and take advantage of the *Routiers* service, although few nationalities compete with the French drivers' intake of wine. Indeed, some foreign drivers believe that French roads are markedly more dangerous in the hours after meal times.

On the French autoroutes, service

tion. European border locations are often situated some way from towns, yet at weekends and holidays the lots are often completely occupied by trucks. Surprisingly there are no comprehensive stops at these sites.

Once out on the road to the Middle East any diesel pump or tea shop is

Truck wash machines (*above*) are a desirable feature of many American stops. Free washes are often provided as a form of discount on other services. With expensive paintwork drivers are keen to keep the rigs looking in good shape. Motels (*right*) frequently give special rates to truck drivers.

facilities such as exist in most countries are often more adventurously designed than the equivalent in Britain or on the eastern US turnpikes. The emphasis is once again on food, and these locations only provide minimal breakdown and service facilities.

In Germany the well-established autobahn system is dotted with Tanken and Rasten stops, where fuel and rest facilities are often complimented by formal dining rooms in addition to snack counters. Most European countries seem to consider the food and fuel aspects to be vital and these are often the only facilities available.

The greatest call for exclusive truck services comes in areas where the road is the only manifestation of civiliza-

likely to attract plenty of truckers, although many of the European stomachs receive no more than home-cooked meals prepared on camping stoves, or the micro-wave ovens fitted in the most sophisticated cabs. If space is available, night-time parking is often to be had for a price, and many truckers will pay to have their safety.

In the wide open spaces of America, the idea of paying for parking space would strike many truckers as extortion. In most large cities, except New York, there are terminals where truckers can lay over while awaiting loads. In Los Angeles, for instance, the truck terminal area is like one giant truck stop comprising several city blocks. The more cramped European cities often ban night-time parking on the streets, and as no comprehensive city terminals exist, other than markets, commercially operated truck parks have become common. These offer nothing more than a space to leave a truck and generally forbid the drivers to sleep in their cabs. These sites, which are often nothing more than day-time car parks, offer the security provided by a guard and the opportunity for drivers to leave their vehicles.

American truckers, it would seem, prefer to stay with their vehicles or at least very close. Lock up and walk away security seldom appeals to them. In fact, when a trucker choses to ride into town, or stay at a regular motel, like a Holiday Inn, he is most likely to drop his trailer somewhere safe and use the tractor as his runabout. The practice of offering security areas in truck stop parks is beginning to grow, although truckers resent the idea of having to pay for the service. One exception might be in New York, where in 1978 plans were drawn up to provide a massive high security truck stop at Hurst Point, close to the Manhattan loading docks. Rather than leave their trucks to the mercy of the New York thieves, truckers had frequently been driving well out of town while waiting for loads. With the new facility as many as 900 trucks at a time will be accommodated behind a high fence, which is patrolled by armed guards and dogs. A motel and repair shop, as well as extensive shopping and recreational facilities, will also be available.

When truck stops can offer such things as a complete truck wash free with a tank full of diesel, or a laundry service, barber shop or a full range of extras and spare parts such as fan belts, filters, wiper blades and mirrors, truckers will linger and spend their money. While aiming to provide what the driver needs for his own well-being, consideration is also given to his equipment, something which rarely occurs in Europe. The Americans' involvement with machinery goes some way to explaining this interest, while the urge to make a buck also plays an important part in motivating the actions of proprietors, because they know only too well that there is another full-service truck stop somewhere just down the road.

THE MAKERS

Bedford. Over 3 million Bedfords have been built since the GMC subsidiary was set up in England in 1931. They now offer a full range of vehicles from the commercial variants of Vauxhall cars, through the ever-popular TK range, to the newest generation of 'muscle trucks'. In the UK Bedford are the third biggest supplier of goods vehicles, after Ford and Leyland. Since the Second World War they have been the major manufacturer of medium-weight trucks for the army, their 4x4 3-ton truck being the basic military vehicle throughout the 1950s and 60s. The recent TM series can be specified for most applications, from 17 tonnes (16.7 tons) to over 42 tonnes (41.3 tons) gvw for heavy haulage units. Detroit Diesel V-8 engines are commonly used.

Berliet. The company began manufacturing automobiles in the last years of the nineteenth century. It made the first purpose-built French truck in 1906. During World War I, Berliet were the major suppliers of military vehicles. In the 1930s they produced their first diesel powered vehicles, thousands of which were supplied with Ricardo-type engines.

Since the early days Berliet have specialized in the heavy end of the truck manufacturing business. Their spacious cab, introduced in 1972, proved to be a popular design and was adopted by Ford for use on their Transcontinental. Heavy Berliets are exported in large numbers particularly to African and Asian countries. A

Heavy-duty Berliets, like this one engaged in logging operations, are the most frequently exported of French trucks. The conventional design *(left)* is well proven and has remained unchanged for many years.

range of off-road and construction vehicles based on the well-proven long-nose design complete the range.

In 1978 a merger with the state-owned Saviem group saw production of the heavier trucks centred on the Berliet factory at Lyons. The Berliet-produced Club of Four models, while sharing the up-dated standard cab, are supplied with their own make of engine. The new series 62030 diesel has been designed to meet all existing emmission regulations with a particular eye on California.

In the heavy range Berliet's most popular engine for long-haul European truckers is the 305 bhp economy diesel, while the most powerful of their highway vehicles is the TR365. This was called the *Centaure* and was the star of the *Salon de Paris*.

DAF. Founded in 1936, van Dorne's Automobilefabriken NV originally built trailers and semi-trailers. They began truck manufacturing in 1950 at Eindhoven. Seven years later they built their own engine and transmission, and since then have made all the major components used in their vehicles. As the only producer of over-the-road trucks in Holland, Dafs are used by most of that country's long haul vehicle operators.

In 1972 Daf entered an arrangement with International Harvester who purchased a 33% holding in the truck division. The top-of-the-line tractive unit is the 2800 model which can be specified for applications up to 56 tonnes gvw. The 38-tonne (37 ton) DKS uses a 305-bhp diesel. For the British market the FT2300 is a 32-tonne (31 ton) powered by a 230-bhp engine. In the UK Daf trucks are the second biggest seller among imported heavy-duty trucks. They also have large export markets in other countries, with assembly plants in Africa and the Middle East.

Diamond Reo was formed in 1971 from two divisions of the White group, Diamond T and Reo. Conventional and cab-over road tractors were built until 1975 when the factory ceased production for over two years. Production began again in 1978, under new management, with a similar range of vehicles.

ERF. The only independent British manufacturer of long-haul trucks other than Foden, ERF, at Sandbach, is the result of a split from the Foden

company in the 1930s. The first model was built in 1933 with a Gardner engine.

In 1974 the B-series replaced the A models, and two years later a sleeper cab version was produced. Gardner, Rolls-Royce and Cummins engines are supplied. The largest 6x4 road tractor is powered by a 350-bhp Cummins and rated at 59-tonnes (58 tons) gvw for TIR work.

Fiat. Fabricca Italiana Automobili Torino built its first truck, a cab-over model capable of hauling 6 tons, in 1904. Today Fiat build a complete range of vehicles from miniature delivery vans to the heaviest construction trucks. They have manufacturing and assembly plants in over 20 countries, including several in South America, Africa and the Middle East.

Along with Unic, Magirus Deutz and OM, Fiat is part of the IVECO group, the combined production of which exceeds that of any other manufacturer in Europe. In 1975 a new series of vehicles was launched, with a standard sleeper cab on the larger models. Although heavy haulage units are manufactured, the prime European long-haul tractor is the 170 model. The 170/35, built for Italy's domestic 44-tonne (43 ton) gvw regulations, is powered by Fiat's own V-8 engine which produces 325 bhp. The gearboxes are American Fullers.

Foden. A long-established British manufacturer which originally built steamers, its first non-steamer was a diesel-powered truck built in the early 1930s. Foden later became best known for its range of 8-wheelers, a type of truck in which Foden still specialize.

In 1977 this independent company from Sandbach, Cheshire, introduced a new range of road tractors which utilized British Motor Panels cabs. Named the Fleetmaster and the Haulmaster these vehicles are available in sleeper or day cab form and can be supplied with Cummins or Rolls-Royce engines up to 290 bhp for the domestic market. Gardner engines can be fitted when less power is required.

Ford. Ford's domination of the American automotive market has extended only through the light-heavyweight class, although in recent years the company have increased their penetration of the long-haul sector. In the early 1960s Ford launched their first series of heavy-duty trucks, powered

either by V-8 gasoline engines or Cummins diesels. In 1966 they introduced the W-series cab-over with integral sleeper. A range of light and medium-heavy conventional trucks, the Louisville series, was introduced in 1970.

In 1978 a new long-haul road tractor replaced the W-series. The CL 9000 featured an all-aluminium aerodynamically designed cab of exceptional lightness, with one of the largest chrome grills seen on an American truck. The cab features a wide sleeper with bumper to back-of-cab length (BBC) of 280cm (110 in). After seven years' design and development the new vehicle marks a serious attempt to woo the owner-operator customer, a market in which

These are two examples of current European production agreements. The Ford Transcontinental (*top*) was introduced in 1975 and has proved to be one of the continents' most popular long-haul trucks. The French-made Unic (*above*) is identical to the Fiat 150 which was first built in the same year.

Ford has lagged behind. The engines most commonly fitted to the CL 9000s are the powerful turbocharged Cummins.

Ford of Europe. Since the establishment of Ford factories in Europe in the 1930s, a range of vehicles have been produced, mainly in the light van and medium truck categories. The Transit van and D-series medium-weight trucks are still in production after many years and several improvements. In Britain more Fords are sold than any other make of commercial vehicle.

In 1975 Ford introduced the Transcontinental series of heavyweight trucks which are built at their Dutch factory. Using a Berliet cab these high-profile long-distance vehicles are the tallest of European trucks, with a height to the cab roof of 3.22m (10ft 7½ ins). Beneath the continental styling the Transconti is an assemblage of American components. Since 1978 a new range of turbocharged Cummins engines rated at up to 370 bhp can be specified, along with Fuller gearboxes and Rockwell rear axles. A long-haul version of the Transcontinental shown in 1976 included all the kitchen and air-conditioning equipment needed on the Middle East run, with such special extras as padlocks on all removeable external items. In 1978 the complete range of Ford commercial vehicles was re-styled, bestowing a newly designed grill on otherwise familiar cab designs.

Freightliner. Founded in 1938 by Consolidated Freightways on America's west coast, Freightliners did not go into production until after the war. The first bubble-nose COEs became a favourite with fleet haulers. The light weight and simplicity of design has changed very little since the models of the early 1950s. At that time trucks were marketed by the White group, and for many years were known as White Freightliners. In 1977 Freightliner assumed control of their own marketing arrangements and offered a new range of tractors. The traditional fleet tractor was joined by the bigger and plusher Power Liner,

A conventional version of the long-lived International Transtar (*left*) was launched in the mid-1970s. The GMC 'crackerbox' (*below*) was a long-lasting design from the 1950s which was replaced by the Astro. The Freightliner (*inset*) is one of Americas most popular Cab-Over models.

aimed at the independents, and for the first time they produced a conventional tractor.

GMC. General Motors, whose main factory is in Pontiac, Michigan, build vehicles of all sizes, and have subsidiary companies in other countries, including Bedford in England. GMC's most significant contribution to contemporary American trucking was the Astro 95 cab-over model, which was introduced in the late 1960s. The Astro, which replaced the square-shaped 'crackerbox' model, was a wind-tunnel-designed tractor, which featured particularly smooth lines, and was the first truck in the world to be offered with an optional roof mounted air deflector, the Dragfoiler. In 1978 a re-designed version, the Astro SS, was introduced. The previous year a conventional tractor, the

General, had been launched and in 1978 was demonstrated with a stand-up walk-in sleeper. The most commonly fitted engines are GMC's own V-6 or V-12 Detroit Diesels.

Chevrolet trucks are identical to the GMC models except for the identifying badges. As Chevrolet specialize in pick-up trucks far fewer of their long haul Titans are sold.

International. Another important company which built its first truck in 1907 and has been the biggest seller of over-the-road trucks since 1944. The Transtar, the basic cab-over model road tractor, is a well-tried vehicle that has been virtually unchanged since the early 1960s. Although it has been re-named the Transtar II, and more recently, the Transtar Eagle, the truck has only undergone minor cosmetic and functional improve-

ments, including a slightly enlarged sleeper cab.

With the introduction of the Eagle in 1977, International also unveiled a conventional version fitted with de-luxe trim and aimed at the owner-operator market. The complete range of American diesel engines can be specified, including Cummins, Caterpillar and Detroit Diesels, as well as International's own V-800 power plant.

Kenworth. Originally manufacturing trucks under the name of Gersix, this company has been building custom trucks in Seattle since 1916. All vehicles are individually built to customer specifications and are mostly over-the-road tractors or off-highway vehicles for use in oil-field work or the lumber industry. Kenworth have a reputation for being the best assemblers of truck components, very few of which they actually make themselves. The company pioneered the use of diesels in heavy American trucks and have been the first to introduce many new ideas, with a keen interest in driver requirements.

In 1975 their VIT series of conventional trucks offered the first walk-in sleeper, with 5ft of headroom, and a 91cm (36 in) bed in a 150cm (60 in) box. Another recent design is the Aerodyne double-deck cab-over, which was the first COE with a raised roof line, which contributed extra space, and also had an aerodynamic function. Since 1945 Kenworth have been a division of Paccar.

Leyland. Originally named the Lancashire Steam Motor Company, the company later took the name of the town in which its factory was established. It is now an autonomous division of the state-owned BL, the major British vehicle producer, having previously absorbed many successful manufacturers of the past, including Albion, AEC and Scammell. The latter is the only division still producing trucks under its original name, many of which are for extra-heavy-duty application, although the Crusader is a highway tractor of up to 40-tonnes (47 tons) gvw. Leyland claim to offer the most comprehensive range of commercial vehicles, from car-based vans to the Marathon long-haul truck. Tippers and rigid trucks in the 16.25 tonne (16 ton) gvw range, along with several bus models, account for most of Leyland's sales in Britain, while many

models are built for export markets.

The Marathon, which was introduced in the mid-1970s, was remodelled as the Marathon 2 in 1977. It can be rated at up to 44 tonnes (43 tons) and, as an alternative to Leyland's own TL diesels, can be specified with Cummins engines. A complete new range of trucks and engines will be unveiled in 1979.

Mack. Probably the most famous name in trucks, with the instantly recognizable bulldog symbol, this company has been a leading manufacturer of heavy and extra-heavy-duty trucks since the earliest days, and was the first US truck builder to supply its own diesel engine.

Mack trucks have extensive worldwide marketing with assembly plants in many countries. In Europe the F-series cab-overs and R-series conventionals have been sold since the Mid-1970s. After their takeover by Mack in the 1950s, Brockway trucks were custom assembled using many Mack parts and proprietary engines. The last model was produced in 1977. The California-built Cruise-Liner, which was introduced in 1975, is the most luxurious of the Mack road tractors, and was particularly designed to catch the eye of the independent truckers. In 1978 a new conventional, the Super-Liner, was added to the range. The Maxidyne engine and Maxitorque transmissions, which Mack developed, are standard equipment on all trucks.

In Europe a 38 tonne (37 ton) version of the F-series cab over has recently been developed. Known as the Eurostater, the model is supplied with 300 bhp Mack diesel.

MAN. Today an autonomous division of Daimler-Benz, in 1915 the MAN company began to build Saurers under licence. Having been an original supporter of Rudolph Diesel, the company continued to develop the engine after his death, and ran the first prototype diesel truck in 1918. Five years later the engine went into production and was used by Mercedes and Saurer.

After the factory was bombed during the Second World War, it was reopened by the Allies in 1945. In 1951 a

The Kenworth *(right)* has the bright-chromed, freshly painted look of the owner-operator's vehicle. The CB radio aerials on either side are attached to the frames for the big, flat 'West Coast' mirrors.

V-8 diesel was built. The present generation of MAN vehicles utilize many components in common with the French Saviem, including the cab, although their own straight six turbocharged diesels are fitted. The 280 model introduced in 1977 proved to be popular with operators in many European countries with its economical engine and low-noise cab. A connection with VW was made in 1978 when plans for a jointly-developed medium truck range were put into action. MAN now also has marketing links with both Saviem and VW.

Marmon. Texas-built trucks, known as a 'rare breed', which are not commonly seen on the American highways. Cab-over and conventional road tractors are built with the usual engine/transmission options. As Marmon-Herrington, the company was one of the early manufacturers of twin-driven tandem axle vehicles.

Mercedes Benz. Part of the giant Daimler Benz organization, which was formed by two of the original pioneers of the internal combustion engine. Daimler Benz is one of the world's largest volume producers of vehicles, with the biggest overall sales of trucks and vans in Europe, and a comprehensive range from light vans to heavyweight trucks. The main truck manufacturing plant is at Wurth, West Germany. Mercedes vehicles are exported to, or assembled in, most countries of the world, including the United States, where medium range diesel-engined trucks have been available for some years. Extensive research and development in the mid-1970s lead to the introduction of the 'low profile' series 16 truck cab, which is adaptable for use on all vehicles from medium-weight 4-wheel rigids to 38 tonne (37 ton) gvw tractors. Their prestige international haulage tractive unit, the 1632 S, utilizes a 10-litre V-10 engine producing 320 bhp.

Oshkosh. This company takes its name from the Wisconsin town where it has manufactured trucks since 1917. Oshkosh vehicles are all specialist and extra-heavy-duty vehicles, used for construction, haulage and oil field work, and as aircraft tenders, tugs, and snow ploughs.

The MAN 280 model *(right)* is marketed in most European countries. Along with Mercedes *(inset)*, MAN was one of the pioneers of the diesel engine.

Peterbilt. Another custom builder, whose vehicles are popular with independent long-haul truckers who appreciate the vehicles' class. Established by T.A. Peterman in California in 1939, the company built its first trucks for the logging industry. In 1958 the firm was absorbed by Paccar. Standard and wide-front conventional road tractors are made, but the biggest of the current series of Peterbilts is the 352H-series cab-over. This is an enlarged version of the traditional cab-over tractor, built to accept large engines like the 450-600 bhp Caterpillar and Detroit engines. It comes with a wide sleeper and a BBC length of 280cm (110 in). Wheelbase, axles and transmissions are to the customer's specifications. A new factory was opened in Tennessee in 1972, and Peterbilt trucks have continued to hold their own in the most competitive section of the market, although still very traditional in many respects.

Peterbilt is a low-volume, high-quality custom truck manufacturer. The trucks are specifically aimed at the American owner-operator. Since 1958 they have been produced by the same company as Kenworth, but both compete for orders in this market.

Saviem. *The Société Anonyme de Vehicles Industriels et d'Equipements Mécaniques* was formed in the mid-1950s by the expansion of Renault's truck division which absorbed several other manufacturers. Among these were Latil and Somua, a group established at the outbreak of World War 1 to build military vehicles. By 1960 Renault had complete control of the group which became its commercial vehicle branch. Renault's first commercial vehicle had been built in 1906, with the first diesel option offered in 1931, but goods vehicles are no longer marketed by them.

The SG range of light and medium trucks introduced by Saviem in the 1950s are still ubiquitous among goods vehicles on French roads and the basic design of the range has remained unchanged into the late 1970s. In 1974, Saviem joined the European Truck Development Group (The Club of Four) with Magirus, Volvo and Daf, and soon became the major partner. The J range used Saviem diesels in light-heavy weights and more powerful MAN engines up to 340 bph in the bigger tractor units. In 1977, home-market Saviems were offered with new MAN D25 engines. These vehicles are almost identical to the MAN 280 and are not available outside France under an agreement with MAN who have had a long standing relationship with Saviem.

The 1978 merger with Berliet under the *Renault Vehicles Industriel* banner established the group as France's only remaining producer of heavy goods vehicles. In the 1980s it is expected that a new range will lead to rationalized production. The best of this range is the RVI middle-range truck to be sold by Mack on the American market.

Scania. A division of Saab-Scania, a company which has been building vehicles since 1897. Scania produce a wide range of medium and heavy-duty trucks utilizing well-tried designs in cab-over and conventional versions, which although unchanged for many years do not appear dated. Along with Volvo, Swedish-built long-haul trucks account for more heavy-duty vehicle sales than Mercedes.

Scania cabs are of all steel construction and their diesel engines are among the quietest and cleanest in the world. In 1978 a new model, the LBS141, was introduced which utilized the familiar cab design, one of the most spacious of European sleepers. The LBS141 is the most powerful vehicle in the Scania range with a new engine rated at 375 bhp. Transmission is by 10-speed synchromesh box.

Seddon Atkinson. Now a subsidiary of International Harvester, this manufacturer uses an amalgamation of

Saviem trucks have recently merged with Berliet to form France's major producer of commercial vehicles. The model above shares many parts in common with the MAN. The rugged-looking logger *(left)* is an Autocar, a make with a long history of building specialist heavy-duty trucks, latterly as a member of the White group.

two old and respected names from the English transport scene. Seddon began building trucks in 1938, while Atkinson had been building steamers since 1914. The current 400 series trucks feature a sleeper cab, and can be fitted with Gardner, Rolls-Royce or Cummins engines. For transcontinental work, diesels of up to 350 bhp can be specified. Complimenting the bigger model are the 300 and 200 medium-weight trucks, which can be fitted with International diesel engines.

Volvo. The Volvo F88/89 series trucks, introduced in the early 1960s, proved to be one of the most popular range of long-haul trucks in Europe. Stringent Swedish construction standards, and the heavier loads hauled on domestic runs, were factors which contributed to the construction of this new generation of trucks, which have been among the top imports in many of the world's markets. In the UK Volvo sell more heavy trucks than any other foreign manufacturer.

The medium-heavyweight F86 model, which was the first to be sold in the UK, has recently been introduced to America, and a new model, the F7, has replaced it in Europe. In 1977 the F88 series was replaced by the new F10 and F12 models, which featured a totally redesigned cab. The new F-series vehicles are available in the

widest range of applications from tippers to sleeper cab 54 tonne tractive units. The top of the range F12 uses a turbocharged TD120C 12-litre engine rated at 350 bhp. N-series conventional trucks are also used extensively in the Swedish lumber industry and on construction work. In 1978 Volvo arranged with Freightliner of America for their dealers to market the Gothenburg-built trucks in the USA.

White. Since 1918 White have been building trucks at factories in Ohio and Virginia. Many other makes have been absorbed by White over the years, including Autocar, Diamond T and Reo. After providing fleet vehicles for many years, White built the Western Star series conventionals in the mid-1970s. This glamorous range was marketed as a separate part of the Big 4 Group, which included White, Western Star, Autocar and Freightliner divisions. The Road Commander COE provided the majority of White sales and was introduced into Europe, reaching Britain in 1978. The same year a new series was introduced to American truckers. A new Western Star cab-over featured a range of custom cabs painted with designs of Indian heads and desert landscapes. The trucks are available with the usual wide range of American optional extras.

INDEX

ACKNOWLEDGEMENTS

The publishers would like to thank the following
organizations and individuals for their kind permission
to reproduce the photographs in this book:

Ardea (Su Gooders) 8 above; American Trucking Association 22
above, 51 above, 80-81; Nick Baldwin 9 above, centre and below,
22 below; Ray Block 27 inset right; Neill Bruce 10-11, 13;
Columbia/EMI/Warner (P. Myers) 66; Ian Dawson 57 above;
Daily Telegraph Colour Library (P. Keen) 79 inset; Helen
Doroshaw 63 below; Editorial Photocolor Archives Inc. 8 below;
Michael Ellis 37; Robert Estall 4-5, 6-7, 11 inset, 14-15, 15 inset,
16, 18-19, 20-21, 27 inset left, 52-53, 67, 86, 87 inset; Graeme
Ewens 26-27, 58-59, 69; Explorer (Anderson-Fournier) 56; Fiat
85 inset; Fleet Owner Magazine 23 below, 24 above; Peter
Fraenkel 55 inset; Sonia Halliday 46 below; Robert
Harding Associates 35, 36; Andy Harris 61, 70-71, 73, 80; The
John Hillelson Agency (Sygma — J. P. Laffont) 61 inset, 62,
64-65, 68 inset; John Mason 72 inset; Mercedes-Benz of North
America 12 above, 90 inset; Michelin Tyre Co. Ltd. 17, 24 below;
Andrew Morland 34 below, 67 inset left and right, 92-93; Tony
Morrison 57 below; Margaret Murray 51 below; Owner Operator
34 above; Martin Phippard 87; Photo Library International —
Leeds 1, 28; The Photographic Library of Australia 30, 44-45, 55;
Renault endpapers, 82-83, 95; Rex Features (M. Garanger) 43,
48-49; Chris Richardson 60, 88-89; Jonathan Roberts 63 above
inset; Ryder Truck Rental, Inc. 23 above, 72; Clive Sawyer 90-91;
John Sims 25, 42, 46 above, 77 above and below, 84-85; Mireille
Vautier (De Nanxe) 50; John Warwick 12 below; Colin
Watmough 32-33, 41 above and below, 52 inset, 76; Andrew
Watson 29; White Motor Corporation 2-3, 38-39, 94; George
Wright 74-75; Ian Moo Young/Moo Movies 68; ZEFA 47.

Picture Research   Zilda Tandy/Mary Corcoran

PDO 79-143